D1569589

Books by Ray Miller

Ray Miller's Houston
Eyes of Texas Travel Guide: Panhandle/Plains Edition
Eyes of Texas Travel Guide: Fort Worth/Brazos Valley Edition
Eyes of Texas Travel Guide: Hill Country/Permian Basin Edition
Eyes of Texas Travel Guide: San Antonio/Border Edition
Eyes of Texas Travel Guide: Dallas/East Texas Edition
Eyes of Texas Travel Guide: Houston/Gulf Coast Edition

Ray Miller's Galveston

RAY MILLER'S
GALVESTON

Library of Congress Catalog Card Number:83-72708
ISBN:0-89123-032-7

Design: John Hillenbrand, Gene Schreiber

Production Art: Gene Schreiber

Set in Century Book II by Kathy Kelley
Printed in the United States of America
by Capital Printing, Austin

FOR VERONICA

CONTENTS

FOREWORD

As developer and guiding light of "The Eyes of Texas" television program for more than a decade, Ray Miller has promoted the cause of Texas history more than perhaps any other Texan, television viewing being what it has become in our modern culture. Traveling to all parts of Texas in search of unique individuals and institutions, Miller discovered more and more history, which he carefully documented for television viewers. In so doing, he developed into a solid historian himself and influenced thousands of others to become more interested in their Texas heritage.

This volume is a welcome addition to recent books on Galveston. Though its place in the development of Texas is unique, Galveston Island has been largely overlooked in written history. One hundred years ago Galveston was the largest, most important city in Texas. Her future seemed boundless. Then came the 1900 storm and everything stopped. Galveston recovered physically from the storm in ten or twelve years, but the city has never recovered psychologically.

Interest in Galveston during this century has centered around the 1900 storm and why Galveston did not remain the metropolis of Texas. In mid-1983, Galveston is on the upswing again and the future is bright with hope.

Although closely connected with Houston for the past forty-five years, Ray Miller is no stranger to Galveston Island. He has maintained a summer home at Jamaica Beach on West Galveston Island for the past twenty years. As the impresario of "The Eyes of Texas" and as manager of the Channel 2 newsroom for twenty years, Miller kept his eye on Galveston. He promoted preservation and restoration eagerly and was at the forefront of media coverage during those days ten and twelve years ago when all historical interests of Galveston were engaged in the fight to preserve and restore Ashton Villa.

I salute Ray Miller for what his career has meant to Galveston. I hope this book about Galveston will enhance his reputation as a Texas historian and do honor to our little sand bar.

Bob Nesbitt
Galveston
August, 1983

INTRODUCTION

"A hick town is a town with no
place to go that you shouldn't."

> Sam Maceo's
> *Galveston Isle Magazine,* 1950

Galveston never qualified as a hick town and Sam
Maceo's enterprises were not the only reason. Geography
gave Galveston some natural advantages. Smugglers have
been taking advantage of them almost from the beginning.
The pirates and privateers and pioneers here all did
whatever they wanted to do for a long time. And some people in Galveston continued to do whatever they wanted to
long after laws were passed against some of the things they
were doing.

Galveston was notorious for bootlegging in the 1920s and
'30s and Galveston was notorious for its wide-open gambling in the 1940s and '50s. But Galveston did not discover
drinking in the 1920s and Galveston did not discover gambling in the 1940s. These activities had been prevalent all over
Texas from the earliest days. Galveston just did not go along
with the new morality when the rest of the state did. Activities that were commonplace everywhere at one time continued to be commonplace here after they had ceased or gone
underground in the rest of Texas.

Very few Galveston people ever were involved in bootlegging, but many Galvestonians bought the bootlegged mer-
chandise. Very few Galveston people actually were involved in gambling. Most of the patrons came from somewhere

Galveston, Texas

Above: *The most popular resort on the seawall in 1927 was the Crystal Palace. It was across 23rd Street from the site where the Buccaneer Hotel was built the following year. The Crystal Palace had arcades and cafes, dressing rooms, a swimming pool and a walkway over the boulevard to the beach.*

Below: *The harbor excursion boat Galvez was based in the 1920s at Pier 21, about where Fisherman's Wharf is today.*

else during the heyday of gambling here, but the gambling houses had a number of employees and paid them well. They paid their taxes and they gave generously to churches and charities. The Galveston attitude toward them was an attitude of cheerful toleration. The major gambling establishments had some ingenius methods of minimizing police interference, but the real reason they prospered as long as they did was that Galvestonians in the main saw no reason why they should not. This attitude was contrary to the prevailing sentiment in Texas. But Galveston never has been embarrassed about being different. And the difference goes far beyond attitudes toward gambling and morals.

Galveston endured the greatest disaster nature ever inflicted on an American city. Galveston lives calmly with the knowledge that it could happen again. Galveston lives as comfortably with its history as any city I know.

The first time I saw Galveston was the summer of 1927. My family brought me down from Fort Worth in a Model T. It was my first long trip. It was the first time I saw a

Opposite top: *The author, on the right, with his father, brother and sister on the beach at Galveston. Not even children went topless on the public beaches in 1927.*

Opposite bottom: *Typical tourists. The Millers took the trip around the harbor on the sightseeing boat Galvez. A better photographer would have tried to get us to look happier. We had more fun than our expressions indicate.*

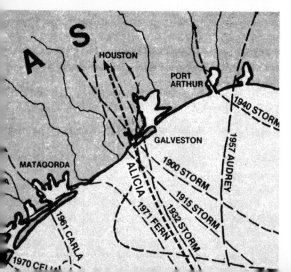

Top: *Some people in Fort Worth thought visiting Galveston was a daring thing to do in 1927. I remember people warning us that we would be killed by a storm or eaten by sharks. I never have come across any evidence of a shark problem here. Evidence of the hurricane problem appears too regularly. What happened to the resort homes on the beach beyond the seawall during Hurricane Alicia in 1983 is evidence of what would happen in Galveston proper if there were no seawall.*

Center: *Galvestonians still must decide early whether they will leave the island or stay when there is a storm approaching. The tides cut off the escape routes usually before it is clear whether the island is going to be directly in the path of an approaching storm. The present causeways never have been damaged by a storm, but the approaches always become impassable. Most Galvestonians have stayed on the island during all the storms Galveston has experienced so far.*

Bottom: *This map shows the paths of the hurricanes that have struck Galveston since 1900.*

body of water I could not see across. It was my first taste of salt water and my first exposure to fresh seafood. I have been partial to salt water and seafood ever since. There were in 1927 some of those places to go that you shouldn't. The Hollywood Club was a popular spot. The Millers didn't go there. I doubt if my mother and dad knew there was such a place. We took the tour on the harbor excursion boat, and I remember my dad speculating about which of the motor-boats we saw might be rumrunners. Everybody knew about the rumrunners.

I have been a part-time resident of Galveston for twenty years. This is long enough to learn the difference between being in Galveston and being a Galvestonian. I write as an acknowledged outsider. I write as an earnest admirer of the town and the spirt of Galveston.

Ray Miller
Jamaica Beach
July, 1983

PART ONE

The Open City 1918-1957

Galveston has many distinctions, but the thing most people have heard most about is the time Galveston was a wide-open town. Galveston's reputation for shady activities probably started on Postoffice Street. A number of respectable families had lived there before, but the houses along Postoffice between 25th and 30th streets were being converted into bawdy houses by the 1890s. The red-light district grew until it spilled over into the side streets and to part of Church Street. The district flourished for more than sixty years.

Some of the houses displayed red lights; others maintained elegant facades. A few houses had girls sitting in the windows in their underwear. The girls wore evening clothes in other houses. The prices varied according to the decor and the girls and the quality of the other amenities. Most had some kind of music. Some had only a player piano or a juke box; others had live music. Most of them had bars. Some attracted sailors; some attracted tired businessmen. Mother Harvey's attracted students. Mother Harvey's was in the 2500 block of Postoffice. This was usually the busiest block in the district.

Most of the bawdy houses had bouncers to keep down the kind of incidents that might attract the police. The district had a reputation as a fairly safe place during its heyday. There were stories about kind-hearted madams safeguarding the valuables of drunken customers. There were stories about customers getting rolled and then recovering their money with the help of the district's own security force.

There were a few houses in the district where only Negro girls worked. The police tried to see to it that these places

This evidently is an ordinary rooming house now. Old timers say it was Mother Harvey's place when this was a wide-open red-light district. The 2500 block of Postoffice Street was lined with similar houses then. This is the only one still standing in what was the busiest block in the district. It has been painted since this picture was made.

were patronized only by Negro men. The police were likely to intervene if they heard that Negro men were trying to do business at one of the other houses. Miscegenation and murder were about the only activities the police concerned themselves with on Postoffice Street in those days.

Granville Price said in a thesis he wrote on Galveston prostitution that sailors had to pay a couple of dollars more than other customers. Some of the town's rich men sometimes threw parties in the bawdy houses.

Glen Campbell was singing in Galveston long before he started singing about Galveston. Campbell tells people he appeared at the Imperial Club on Postoffice Street when he was fourteen years old. That would have been about 1952. The Imperial was about two blocks outside the red-light district.

The open prostitution lasted longer than the bootlegging and the open gambling. The bootlegging started about 1918 with Prohibition. Repeal of the 18th Amendment ended it. Big league gambling started about 1925. Texas Attorney General Will Wilson's intervention in 1957 ended it and most of the open prostitution, too.

Some people always thought the madams on Postoffice Street must have been paying off the police. One police chief claimed payoffs never were necessary because what the people on Postoffice Street were doing was an accepted part of the Galveston scene. It probably was true that Galveston got the kind of law enforcement Galveston wanted.

Galveston city and county lawmen often said in the 1940s and 1950s that the people wanted open gambling. They had it. Sam and Rose Maceo were the names everybody knew. They were the biggest operators. They never were the only operators.

Sam and Rose were born in Sicily. They were still children when their parents migrated to Leesville, Louisiana. Sam and Rose moved to Galveston in 1910. They went to barber school and both got jobs in the barber shop at the new Galvez Hotel.

The Maceo brothers switched from barbering to bootlegging when Prohibition began. Their original partner in the bootlegging business was Dutch Voight. He was also a member of their gambling syndicate. The syndicate started moving into the speak-easy business in 1926. The Maceos bought a small restaurant on a pier off the seawall at 21st Street. It had been known previously as Chop Suey. The syndicate changed the name to Maceo's Grotto. It was later called Sui Jen.

Ollie Quinn had opened the more elaborate Hollywood Dinner Club and speak-easy on Stewart Road at 61st Street.

Top: *The Hollywood Dinner Club was one of the places where the great entertainers appeared during the Prohibition period. The club was started by others, but Sam and Rose Maceo bought into it by the time it opened or shortly afterward. The Maceos already were prosperous bootleggers.*

Bottom: *The Maceo brothers' first venture into the business was a restaurant on a pier over the Gulf at 21st Street. It had been called Chop Suey before they bought it. The Maceos operated it under a couple of other names before they decided to call this place the Balinese Room. It was the most famous gambling resort in Texas for almost twenty years.*

5

The site was just outside the Galveston city limits at the time. Gambler Jakie Freedman bought a piece of the club. He sold out to the Maceos and moved to Houston to open a gambling resort on South Main. The Maceos made the Hollywood Club a showplace. It was the first air-conditioned night club in America. It could seat 500 people for dinner. There were crap tables, blackjack tables and roulette wheels. There was live entertainment by the biggest names in show business.

Rose Maceo never was known for his social skills. Sam had all the charisma in the family. He blossomed as the host of the Hollywood Club. He traveled to Hollywood to book shows for the club. He became friendly with the stars and he treated everyone like a star.

The Maceos did not tolerate boisterous conduct in any of their clubs and they had plenty of bouncers to maintain decorum. They served fine food and drinks. The service was outstanding and the prices were moderate. There never was any pressure on the customers to visit the gambling rooms, but the Maceos did not let just anybody in them, either. They knew who was likely to gamble. They were especially partial to oilmen and rich Jews from Houston. Sam tried to see to it that there were enough waiters with cigarette lighters so that no guest had to light his own cigarette or cigar.

Ben Bernie, Guy Lombardo, the Boswell Sisters, Glen Gray, Phil Harris, Paul Whiteman, Joe Reichman, Henry Busse, Shep Fields, Henry King, Jack Teagarten, Richard Himber, Herbie Kay, Spike Jones and Duke Ellington all played the Hollywood Dinner Club. The NBC radio network often picked up thirty minutes or an hour of entertainment

Opposite: *The Maceo
brothers both were dead by the
time Attorney General Will
Wilson and Sheriff Paul
Hopkins called a halt to the
gambling in Galveston. The
Maceos' successors tried to
operate the Balinese Room as a
dinner club without much
success. The place was damaged
by Hurricane Carla and closed
for five years before oilman
Johnny Mitchell bought it.
Mitchell has been operating the
Balinese Room as a dinner
theater since 1966. He says it is
not making any money. The food
end of the business never made
any money when the Maceos were
in charge, either.*

Above: *Sam Maceo, on the left,
entertaining General Jimmy
Doolittle and Mayor Herb
Cartwright in the Balinese
Room. Sam was the front man
for the Maceo syndicate from the
beginning until he died in 1951.
He was always immaculately
and expensively dressed. He was
pleasant and courteous and he
was very well liked.*

7

from the Hollywood Club on Saturday nights. One account says the first live remote musical program ever heard on network radio came from the Hollywood Club. The performers were Ben Bernie and All the Lads. The existence of the Hollywood Club certainly was no secret. Many people knew that more than dinner and dancing went on there. Many others guessed. Not many people worried about it. The club sat well back off the road behind a fence. But raiding officers could drop in fairly readily. They did that one day in 1939 and afterwards they got an injunction and had the Hollywood Club padlocked.

The Maceos learned a few lessons from that experience. They expanded the Sui Jen on the pier out over the Gulf. They decorated it like a South Seas resort and they changed the name to the Balinese Room. The place had the same attractions the Hollywood Club had. There was good food, good music and plenty of drinks. There was a back room with slot machines and gaming tables. There was the famous Maceo hospitality, and something else. The Balinese Room was almost raid-proof. Anyone entering the place had to stop first at a door right off the seawall. The doorman at this outer door relayed the names of the arriving guests by telephone or intercom to a doorman out at the Balinese Room itself. He did not open the outer door until he had an okay from the man at the main door. A Texas Ranger might barge past the man at the outer door, of course, but it would take him a little time to get to the main door, even if he ran all the way. The man at the outer door would have sounded an alarm in the meantime. The people on duty in

the gambling room would have plenty of time to convert the crap tables into pool tables and the blackjack tables into bridge tables. They could hide the slot machines or throw them into the water if they had to before any raider could make his way through the restaurant into the back room.

The Balinese Room became the most fashionable restaurant in Galveston. Celebrities visited the place and shared a table with smiling Sam Maceo. Public officials and military officers were often seen there. They were often photographed there. The pictures sometimes appeared in the newspapers. No one thought anything of it, except the Texas Rangers and a few people in Austin. The Rangers came to the island in the spring of 1938 and explained the law to Sheriff Frank Biaggne. The sheriff and Police Chief Tony Messina issued a public notice advising gamblers to close down. They even made a few arrests. Mayor Adrian Levy ordered the slot machines removed from public restaurants, drug stores and other public places. But the serious gambling never stopped.

Opposite: *Rose Maceo, on the right, was Sam's brother and partner. He concerned himself more with the details of their business and let Sam have the limelight.*

Right: *Bob Hope may have been kidding Sheriff Frank Biaggne, when this picture was made, about Biaggne's claim that he could not raid the Balinese Room because he was not a member and they wouldn't let him in. Biaggne was sheriff during most of the open gambling era.*

This was several years before Sheriff Biaggne achieved a measure of fame by telling a legislative committee he had not raided the Balinese Room because it was a club, he was not a member and they would not let him in.

The Maceos were making big money in the 1920s and '30s. They thought they might build a hotel to accommodate their customers. They never built it. People said the town's leading citizen told them not to. The leading citizen was W. L. Moody, Jr. He and his family had made millions in cotton, banking and insurance. The Moodys entered the hotel business in 1927. They built the Jean Laffite downtown that year and they built the Buccaneer on the seawall in 1928. W.L. Moody, Jr. may have let the Maceos know he would not welcome competition, but there is no record of it, of course.

The Moodys eventually had dozens of hotels around the country and all three of the principal hotels in Galveston. W.L. Moody, Jr. bought the Galvez in 1941. Sam Maceo was living in the Galvez penthouse at the time. Phil Harris was

Left: *Sam Maceo lived in hotels until 1950. He and his second wife had three children by then and Maceo built them a home. He admired a house Frank Sinatra was living in at the time. He imported Sinatra's architect from Palm Springs and had him build this house in the Cedar Lawn subdivision. Sam Maceo died before the house was finished. His family lived here briefly and then moved to Louisiana*

Opposite: *The Balinese Room was the liveliest spot on the seawall in the 1930s,1940s and 1950s. There was a line of expensive cars from Houston parked on the boulevard outside the entrance every night.*

married to Alice Fay in the Maceo penthouse in 1941. Harris told me they actually had been married in Tijuana a couple of weeks before, but Alice was not sure it was legal. There was some question whether her divorce from Tony Martin was final. They wanted to have another ceremony. Sam Maceo invited them to have it at his place because Sam had been married to dancer Edna Sedgewick at Harris' home in California earlier the same year. Sam and Edna left the Galvez when the Coast Guard took it over in World War II. They moved to the Buccaneer and eventually built a home in the exclusive Cedar Lawn subdivision.

Sam Maceo had to go to New York in 1942 to defend himself in federal court. A government informant had accused him of dealing in narcotics. Few people in Galveston believed it. The jury in New York was not convinced, either. Maceo was acquitted after Phil Harris testified that he and Sam were together somewhere else when the narcotics sale supposedly was made. Harris said it was just a case of a convicted user making up a story to try to earn a lighter

The Maceos paid their respects to their tolerant fellow citizens by having their high-priced entertainers put on free concerts on the seawall on Sundays. Phil Harris and his band are performing here on Murdock's Pier in 1939.

sentence. He said the case cost Maceo a million dollars. Sam surely made that back after World War II, if not before.

The Maceo clubs had some really big years right after the war. Prohibition was over, but people still could not get mixed drinks anywhere in Texas except in places like their clubs. There were such places elsewhere and some of them had gambling, too. But the Maceo clubs drew big spenders from Houston, Dallas, Fort Worth, Oklahoma, Kansas and places even farther away because they were famous. They were also regarded as clean operations. It was said the Maceos were so jealous of their reputation that they would send escorts to make sure any big winners got home safely with their winnings. Many noted Houstonians were regulars at the Maceo tables. Oilman R.H. Abercrombie testified in court in 1960 that he once lost $31,000 in one night at the Balinese Room. Abercrombie was not claiming this was a record. He was just identifying a check government tax men had found in the syndicate files. The government filed several tax suits against members of the Maceo syndicate after the clubs closed. Abercrombie was called as a witness in one of the suits.

A few rich Galvestonians were regulars in the Maceo clubs, but the syndicate never tried very hard to get islanders to the tables. They might lose more then they could afford and develop bad feelings. The Maceos could do what they were doing only as long as Galveston citizens had good feelings about them. They cultivated good feelings with big contributions to churches and charities and assorted good causes. They had their big name entertainers put on free public concerts on the seawall. Sam personally brought a troupe of Hollywood stars in to do a benefit for the people of Texas City after the explosion there in 1947. He was one of the most popular men in Galveston.

I saw Sam Maceo only a couple of times. I never saw Rose. A friend of mine was a friend of Vic Fertitta. My friend took me to the Maceo clubs several times in the late 1940s. Vic Fertitta and his brother, Anthony, were nephews of Sam and Rose Maceo. Anthony helped run the Balinese Room. Vic was working at the Studio Lounge downtown. The Studio Lounge, the Western Room and the Maceo offices were above the Maceo's Turf Grill in the 2200 block of Market Street.

The Turf Grill was open twenty-four hours a day and it was open to anybody. People went there to make bets on ball games and horse races more often than they went there to eat. The big spenders went upstairs on an elevator that was just inside the entrance. There was always a Maceo man on duty at the elevator door. Sometimes it was Vic Fertitta. He saw to it that only the right people got on the elevator, but if the wrong people somehow got on, it was not a disaster. The elevator was very slow. It was so slow that, when the man on duty sounded the alarm, the men upstairs had plenty of time to get rid of the evidence before any unwelcome visitors could get through the dining room to the gaming room.

I never saw it happen, but people said when there was a signal that law officers were coming into one of the clubs, the band would strike up "The Eyes of Texas." Many diners would stand up and this would create a little extra difficulty for the raiders.

I never paid for anything I ate or drank at the Balinese Room or the Studio Lounge. I never saw my friend pay either. I don't think there was ever a check. The Maceos were famous for laying on free food and drink for people in the news business. It was a very effective part of their public relations program, but they did not include obscure radio reporters in it. I was just a friend of one of their friends. They apparently did not charge their friends. I doubt very much if the restaurant end of their business ever broke even. I was off duty anytime I was in one of the Maceo places, of course. I never made any reports on my radio news programs about there being gambling in those places. This may be difficult for some people to understand today. I will not claim I was right not to tell, but it was not until Marvin Zindler discovered the Chicken Ranch at La Grange in 1973 that reporters started doing news reports about things everybody already knew.

Mayor Herbert Cartwright told a public meeting of a legislative investigating committee in 1951 that gambling and prostitution were out in the open in Galveston. He said it was the best way because undercover gambling and prostitution could breed gang wars.

Several members of the Houston City Council got some unwanted publicity one day in 1952 because they were in the Balinese Room when the Rangers dropped in. The Rangers didn't find any gambling, of course.

Sam Maceo was dead by this time. He died of cancer at

Opposite: *Herbert Y. Cartwright, Jr. was mayor of Galveston during most of the open gambling era. He held the office from 1947 until 1955 and again from 1959 until 1960. Cartwright would tell anybody that Galveston had open gambling. He was openly friendly with the people running the gambling clubs.*

Above: *Sophie Tucker came back to Galveston in 1956 to play an engagement at the Balinese Room that had originally been scheduled for 1953. The original engagement had to be cancelled because of a fire that damaged the famous gambling resort on the eve of Sophie's scheduled opening.*

Johns Hopkins in 1951. His widow and their three small children moved away. Rose Maceo headed the syndicate until he died in 1954. The Fertitta brothers ran things after that. The Balinese Room was closed temporarily in 1952. It was open again in 1953 and Sophie Tucker was just about to begin an engagement when the place caught fire. Sophie lost most of her baggage in the blaze. The club was repaired. It opened again in 1956 with Sophie Tucker as the star attraction.

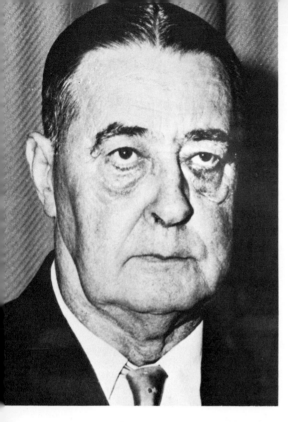

George Clough was mayor of Galveston by this time. He disagreed with Herb Cartwright about a lot of things, but he agreed that Galveston should be an open city. Clough made it pay for the city. He had the police make a few raids on the houses in the red-light district. He made it plain he was not trying to close them. He said the raids would be made once a month. The madams would be fined $100 dollars each and the girls would pay $25 each. The mayor said the city could make about $1,000 a month this way and the people in the district did not object. They could go right back to work. Clough said he and the madams had a working agreement. He told me in a news conference on television that this was a whole lot better than having the girls freelancing all over town. He said the police had orders to arrest any girls they found working outside the district. Clough drew a lot of criticism, but he was reelected in 1957. He was in office when the town was closed, but he did not close it.

George Clough said his reelection proved that Galveston still wanted an open city, but Sheriff Frank Biaggne lost his office the same year. Paul Hopkins was elected sheriff. He had promised in his campaign that he would enforce the laws in Galveston. Will Wilson won the state attorney general's office with the same kind of promise. Wilson took office in January, 1957. He said he would wait until spring to see if the local officials in Galveston would do anything. Sheriff Hopkins made a raid on a club in Kemah in February and seized some liquor and gambling equipment. He did not make any promises when reporters asked him whether he would raid the Balinese Room.

Will Wilson came to the island the first of May and made a speech to the Rotary Club at the Galvez Hotel across the street from the Balinese Room. He urged local officials to enforce the laws. He promised that the state would do it if they did not. Mayor Clough said it was a nice talk but mostly political ballyhoo.

Sheriff Hopkins showed up in the Turf Grill the evening of May 30, 1957, and announced that he wanted to go up to the Studio Lounge. Vic Fertitta went up with him. The system was working fine. The elevator moved very slowly. The men on duty upstairs got the signal, but a couple of the gamblers flashed badges and stopped the staff from clearing away the gambling gear. The two gamblers were deputy sheriffs Hopkins had planted. Charges were filed against the manager of the gaming room and the bartender.

The attorney general was following a similar plan. He had hired a couple of refinery workers from Texas City. He disguised them as high rollers. They talked their way into the Western Room downtown. They lost some money there

Frank Sinatra enjoying a night out with Anthony Fertitta at the Balinese Room in 1950. Sinatra was the headliner at the Shamrock in Houston at the time.

and they were soon being allowed in the Balinese Room. Wilson began assembling a force of Rangers and state prosecutors in Houston in early June. He was planning simultaneous raids on the major gambling houses in Galveston, Brazoria and Fort Bend counties. Somebody tipped off Anthony Fertitta. All the clubs in the three counties closed their gambling rooms the night of June 6. The men Wilson had planted notified him. The raids were cancelled. Evidence gathered by the two refinery workers enabled Wilson to get an injunction against the Balinese Room. The gambling room there closed for good.

The attorney general's crew and the sheriff's men started a series of raids on places where they believed gambling equipment had been stored. They found 550 slot machines in some old buildings at Fort Travis on Bolivar Point. The machines were smashed in the presence of news cameras. More machines were seized from a Maceo syndicate garage on 25th Street. The raiders hit the jackpot the night of June 19. They raided the old Hollywood Club. It had been closed

Opposite: *Will Wilson won the state attorney general's office in 1956. He was orchestrating a major campaign against the gambling resorts by the middle of 1957. Wilson is pictured here, on the right, with Johnny Klevenhagen of the Texas Rangers.*

Above: *Phil Harris and Alice Fay came back to Galveston for the festivities when the Balinese Room re-opened as a dinner theater in 1966. They had been married in Galveston in 1941. Harris and his orchestra had played in the Maceo clubs. He and Sam Maceo were good friends.*

Above: *Several Maceos live in Galveston still. Ronnie Maceo is the grandson of one of Sam's and Rose's cousins. Ronnie runs an oyster bar on Postoffice Street and he has been collecting mementoes of the Maceo period. The menu he is holding is from the Studio Lounge. The furniture is from the Turf Grill. Ronnie Maceo also has the bar from the Turf Grill and a little gambling equipment.*

Left: *Al Scharff had several encounters with the Maceo brothers during Prohibition. Scharff was the customs agent in Galveston. He helped send some of the bootleggers to prison, but he could not get a jury to believe the Maceos were doing anything wrong.*

20

for years, but the raiders found 1,000 slot machines and pin-ball machines there. The raiders broke up the machines. They burned some of them. They hauled the others out and dumped them in the harbor.

Mayor Clough complained to the Army Corps of Engineers that dumping anything in navigable waters without permission was against the law. The Corps did not take any action against the attorney general.

Anthony Fertitta was convicted of permitting gambling when he was tried in 1959 in the case Will Wilson made from the testimony of the two refinery workers. Fertitta got a suspended sentence. He worked for a while in Las Vegas. He managed the Cork Club for Glenn McCarthy in Houston for a time in the early 1960s. He now lives in Louisiana. Vic Fertitta died in 1960 before his gambling case came to trial.

The Will Wilson crusade also brought on the closing of the red-light district.

The old Hollywood Club burned August 13,1959. There is a Gulf self-service gas station now where the main gate was. The Balinese Room was badly damaged in 1961 by Hurricane Carla. It was closed for a long time. It is a dinner theater now, without gambling.

Almost all the old bawdy houses have been torn down. Herb Cartwright and George Clough are dead. Sam and Rose are gone. Galveston has no more vice now than the average American city.

Some people still think of the Maceo days as the good old days. Sam's legend is still growing. He was respected more than he was feared. One of his principal adversaries even had a grudging respect for Sam. The late customs agent Al Scharff believed that Sam Maceo saved his life. Scharff said another bootlegger twice brought in gunmen to kill him. He said Sam personally saw to it that the gunmen left town.

Several reports credit Sam Maceo with getting word to the police any time agents of any outside syndicate showed up on the island. Many Galvestonians believed that whatever the Maceos were doing, they probably were preventing somebody else from doing something worse.

The climate is less ideal than the
ads circulated in the early
twentieth century claimed, but it
is benign. Galveston usually has
the coolest temperatures in Texas
in the summer months and the
warmest temperatures in the
winter months.

Top: *A large part of the Gulf shrimp fleet is based at Galveston.*

Left: *Galvestonians avoid many of the island's tourist attractions. But many of them dress in old English costumes and mingle with the visitors during the Dickens's Evening on The Strand in December.*

Opposite right: *The Port of Galveston operates its own rail switching network and maintains its own railroad repair shop.*

Above: *Architect Howard Barnstone said this church looks like something designed by a pastry cook, but it is a favorite of photographers and artists. This is Sacred Heart at 14th Street and Broadway.*

Top: *The Port of Galveston was developed by a syndicate of entrepreneurs. The City of Galveston bought it in 1940.*

Left: *Part of the light that floods the sanctuary of Trinity Episcopal Church in the day time filters through a Tiffany window.*

Opposite right: *Unobstructed
views of sunrise and sunset are
spectacular surprises for visiting
city dwellers.*

Above: *Commercial fishing is
one of the mainstays of the
Galveston economy. Joe Grillo is
a shrimper.*

Above: *Catamarans have become very popular with Galvestonians and visitors, too, because they can be launched just about anywhere.*

Opposite top: *Galveston was the first important seaport in Texas. Many Galvestonians still earn their living on the waterfront.*

Opposite left: *Many of the unusual shells offered for sale on Seawall Boulevard are imported. The sand dollars are natives.*

Right: *The sights along the Galveston waterfront are best seen from the waterside. Excursion boats offering tours of the harbor are based at Pier 19.*

Top: *The last Galveston scene Houstonians see on their way back to the city on Sunday night is the endless stream of tail lights on the causeway.*

Left: *Galvestonians resented them in the beginning, but they have grown accustomed to the sight of oil rigs off their island.*

Opposite center: *Galveston's weather is at its best in September. The worst storms usually occur in September, too. Alicia struck in August, the day after this photograph of the Galveston beachfront was made.*

Above: *Shrimp boat owners decorate their boats with paper flowers once each spring for the ceremony where the Catholic bishop or a clergyman acting for him bestows the church's blessing upon the shrimp fleet.*

Above: *Cadets at the Texas Maritime College on Pelican Island learn that some of the jobs connected with the maritime business are decidedly lacking in glamour.*

Opposite top: *The bark Elissa went sailing in the Gulf of Mexico on Labor Day in 1982 after she was restored by the Galveston Historical Foundation.*

The Elissa has been berthed at Pier 21 since then, but the foundation plans to take her on other sea trips from time to time.

Opposite left: *Mainlanders acquainted with shrimp only the way they look on the table are surprised to find they are a much less appetizing color as they come off the boats.*

Right: *Galveston has lost a number of significant landmarks to fire over the years. The most recent victim was the old Washington Hotel. George Mitchell was preparing to restore the building when it burned August 26, 1983. Mitchell is thinking of rebuilding it.*

Top: *The Galveston Historical Foundation decorates Ashton Villa for the Christmas Holidays and stages parties on the lawn to celebrate the Fourth of July. The old mansion has been carefully restored, inside and out.*

Left: *The Grand Opera House in the 2000 block of Postoffice is being restored by the Cultural Arts Council.*

Opposite right: *The most conspicuous home on Broadway is also one of the city's stoutest buildings. The house Nicholas Clayton designed for the Walter Greshams in 1886 has withstood every hurricane since.*

Above: *One of these container cranes was wrecked by Hurricane Alicia in August, 1983.*

Above: *Most of the buildings along the beach suffered some damage in the 1983 hurricane. Some of the newer apartment and condominium complexes on Seawall Boulevard were heavily damaged. The sturdy old Galvez Hotel lost some of its windows and part of its roof.*

Opposite top: *The worst damage occurred on the west end of the island where there is no seawall.*

Opposite left: *Most of the residents of the city stayed in Galveston during the storm. But all of the resort subdivisions on the west end fortunately were evacuated.*

Right: *Seagulls ride the wind far inland during Gulf hurricanes. They always come back. Galvestonians do too, but they know that a storm worse than Alicia may come any September.*

PART TWO

The Early Years 1500-1821

It is not certain which Indian tribe first became aware of the island now called Galveston. The Karankawa were the Indians on the scene when the first European reached here. Some historians believe the Karankawa actually lived on the mainland and came to the island only to hunt and fish and bury their dead. Evidence that it was a burying ground was discovered by Willie Holliday on November 12, 1962. Holliday was an employee of the Jamaica Beach subdivision on the west end of the island. He turned up a few bones and a skull. The word spread and amateur archaeologists swarmed in. There was some professional investigation, too. Dr. Tom Pulley of the Museum of Natural Science in Houston identified the bones as Karankawa remains.

The Spanish explorers Juan de Grijalva and Alonso Alvarez de Pineda passed this way in 1519 and 1520. They noted the presence of the island, but they did not stop. The first Europeans to set foot on the island had no intention of doing so. This happened in the fall of 1528. The Europeans were Spaniards. They had come to this part of the world with an expedition headed by Panfilo de Narvaez. They planned to start a colony somewhere on the Gulf. They landed at Tampa Bay and split up there. Part of the party stayed with the ships and eventually went back to Spain. Some of the party stayed ashore until they became convinced they had missed their intended rendezvous with the ships. The stranded Spaniards built some crude boats and set out for the coast of Mexico. A storm washed two of the boats ashore on an island. Many historians believe the island was

Opposite: *Bernardo de Galvez was viceroy of Mexico in 1786 when Spanish map makers under his direction surveyed the Texas coast. The map makers named the biggest bay on the coast for Galvez. The name was later applied by others to the settlement on the island protecting the bay. Galvez never was here.*

41

Galveston. It is generally accepted in Galveston that it was this island and that the first European to step ashore was Alvar Nunez, known as Cabeza de Vaca. There were about eighty Spaniards stranded here, but Cabeza de Vaca apparently was the one with the most rank. He had been treasurer of the Narvaez expedition. He survived to write an account of his experiences that got into the history books. Most of his companions died of exposure during the winter of 1528. Cabeza de Vaca and three others managed to stay alive. One of the other survivors was a Moor called Estevanico. It is generally believed that he was the first black to reach Texas. Cabeza de Vaca and Estevanico knew enough about medicine to make a few sick Indians feel better. This and Estevanico's color made it possible for the stranded Spaniards to pass themselves off to the Indians as supernatural folks. So the Indians helped them along their way and they made it to Mexico about eight years after they made their unscheduled landing here.

Cabeza de Vaca regarded being here as a considerable misfortune. The island accordingly was called *Malhado* in some journals and on some charts for a time. All the early accounts agreed there was a surplus of snakes on the island. This is the reason the island showed up on some early charts as *Isla de Culebras,* or Island of Snakes.

The French explorer Robert La Salle made several trips around Texas after he landed at the mouth of the Lavaca River in 1685 and before he was killed by his own men near the present town of Navasota in 1687. La Salle was lost and trying to find his way to Louisiana, or he was scouting out the Spanish presence in this part of New Spain. It depends upon which version you believe. La Salle was in the habit of naming places he found in honor of Louis XIV. He may have named this island for Louis. This could explain the name of the pass at the west end of the island. San Luis is the Spanish spelling of Saint Louis.

The name of the Galvez family is the name that finally stuck, but no member of the Galvez family ever was here. Matia de Galvez was viceroy of Mexico in the 1780s. He was the father of Bernardo de Galvez. Bernardo was governor of Louisiana when Spain held Louisiana during the American Revolution.Bernardo assisted the American colonists with their revolt. He also commissioned a survey of the Texas coast. The surveyors named the biggest bay they found for Bernardo de Galvez. Bernardo succeeded his father as viceroy of Mexico in 1786. The Spanish were meticulous cartographers. The bay was marked with the Galvez name on every Spanish chart and it was known by that name when Louis-Michel Aury landed here in 1816. Aury was French.

Developer Johnny Goyen was extending his Jamaica Beach subdivision on West Galveston Island in 1962 when one of his employees dug into an Indian burial ground. Goyen, shown here with his sons, John and Bobby, fenced off the area and called in an archaeologist.

Right: *The remains discovered in the burial ground at Jamaica Beach were identified as those of Karankawa Indians. Some of them were displayed for a while in the Galveston County Museum, but museums don't display Indian remains much anymore.*

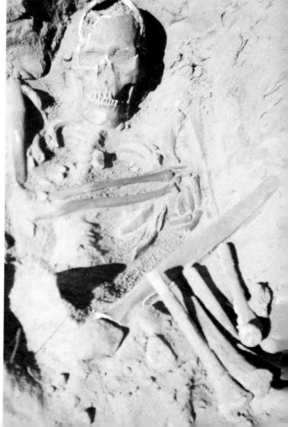

He had been operating a fleet of privateers in the Gulf and the Caribbean. He had also joined one of several American groups plotting to take Mexico away from Spain. Aury established a base on the island. He was probably the original smuggler here. Valuables his privateers seized on the high seas were smuggled into New Orleans. The first gambling probably started about this time, too.

Aury's political allies proclaimed his base a port of the purported Republic of Mexico. Soon another fleet showed up in Galvez Bay. It was commanded by Francisco Xavier Mina. He was a non-conforming Spaniard. He left Spain in a hurry after his attempt to overthrow Ferdinand VII failed in 1814. Some Mexican liberals and Americans he met in England encouraged Mina to mount an expedition against the Spanish rule in Mexico.

Many Americans were eager to meddle in the affairs of the Spanish colony. Mina was able to acquire eight ships and recruit 235 men by visiting Washington, Baltimore, Philadelphia, Norfolk and New Orleans. Mina had given

Left: *A young Spanish revolutionary named Francisco Mina rashly tried to capture Mexico in 1817. He used Galveston Island as a base for the venture that ended when Spanish troops captured him and executed him.*

Opposite: *The notorious privateer Jean Laffite practically ruled Galveston Island for about four years until the U.S. Navy made him leave in 1821.*

himself the title of general by the time he joined Aury on this island on November 22, 1816.

Colonel Henry Perry and another 100 American volunteers joined Aury and Mina here in March, 1817. Perry had intruded on Spanish territory before. He was an officer with the Gutierrez-Magee expedition in 1812. He had control of San Antonio for a little while and he was lucky enough to escape when the Spanish took it back on August 18, 1813.

Mina, Aury and Perry made their move in April, 1817. Relations among them evidently were never very cordial and they were soon going their separate ways. Aury escorted Mina's ships to the Mexican coast and then sailed back here. Mina and Perry could not agree on where to start the war. Perry wanted to attack Texas. Mina wanted to attack Mexico. Perry took his troops and marched off toward Goliad, while Mina captured Soto la Marina. Both were dead before the end of the year. Francisco Mina was captured by Spanish troops, taken to Mexico City and executed on November 11. Perry lost half his force before he reached Goliad, but he

Left: *Jim Bowie probably visited Galveston while Laffite was running things here. He probably bought slaves the privateers had captured and smuggled them into Louisiana.*

Opposite: *The wording on the stone marker the state put up in 1936 in a grove of oak trees on West Galveston Island suggests that the grove was the site of Jean Laffite's headquarters. The pirates may have had a camp here at one time and they may have had a fight with the Karankawa Indians here, but this was not the Laffite headquarters.*

boldly demanded on June 18 that the Presidio la Bahia be surrendered to him. The Spanish troops instead surrounded his party and attacked. Perry killed himself on June 19 to avoid being captured.

Aury had left a very small party at his base here when he sailed off with Mina and Perry. Jean and Pierre Laffite moved in and took over the base while Aury was away. They recruited the few followers Aury had left behind. They were in firm charge of the place when Aury returned. Aury stayed around for a few weeks, then left in July to set up a new privateering base on an island off Nicaragua.

The Laffite brothers initially called their camp Campeche. It was sometimes spelled Campeachy. Some reports say the name Galvezton originally was applied to another settlement on the bay. Jean Laffite probably was the first to apply the name to this place. The name began to show up in documents and journals in 1817 and 1818. Galvezton eventually became Galveston and the name eventually was applied to the island, too.

Jean and Pierre Laffite were French. They probably were also Spanish agents. The Laffites probably were born in Haiti; Jean about 1782 and Pierre about four years earlier. Some accounts say Pierre was smarter, but Jean evidently was the front man. Charisma had not become an industry yet. People had only as much as they were born with. Jean Laffite was born with more than most.

The Laffites were in Louisiana by 1804. The brothers were running a prosperous smuggling business out of a base at Barataria there by 1808. They bought shares in privateers and eventually acquired privateers of their own. They were also involved in some of the plotting to upset the Spanish rule in Mexico. Governor W.C.C. Claiborne of Louisiana broke up the smuggling base at Barataria in 1814. The British proposed to the Laffite brothers that they join the British invasion of Louisiana. The Laffites reported the proposition to U.S. authorities in New Orleans. They then helped Andrew Jackson repel the British attack. This generated some kindly feelings. The Laffites suggested that

the U.S. might return the favor by making Governor Claiborne give them back the property they lost at Barataria. President James Madison decided the government did not owe the pirates that much. That's when the Laffite brothers decided to move to Texas.

The Laffites were privateers.The people they captured and robbed at sea seldom appreciated the difference, but privateers were not quite the same as pirates. Pirates stopped ships, killed people and stole things on their own account. Privateers were licensed by a government to prey on the ships of other nations. The major powers swore off licensing privateers in 1856, but in 1818 any enterprising pirate could find some government to grant him the letters of marque that would make him a privateer.

The Laffites owned some ships outright. They also allowed other privateers to use their base in exchange for a share of their loot. They controlled Galveston Island for about four years. They probably had about 1,000 people here. It was Spanish territory, but it was almost an independent state and Jean Laffite ran it from his headquarters in a big house he built on the waterfront. One of Laffite's enterprises was smuggling slaves into Louisiana. One of the smugglers he dealt with was James Bowie. Laffite's followers were the first to learn how vulnerable Galveston is to hurricanes. A major storm wrecked part of their settlement and part of their fleet in the fall of 1818.

An unemployed French general named Charles Lallemand came here in 1818 and asked the Laffites to help him set up a settlement on the mainland. Lallemand was one

The site known as Laffite's Grove was a popular picnic spot in the 1800s when this picture was made. The site is privately owned now and fenced in. The public is not welcome.

of Napoleon Bonaparte's supporters. Napoleon was in exile. Most historians agree that Lallemand's idea was to create a base that might be used for a campaign to capture Mexico. He apparently hoped to install Joseph Bonaparte as king of Mexico and then mount a campaign from there to put Napoleon back in power in France. The Bonapartes and their followers seldom dreamed small dreams.

Jean Laffite sold the Lallemand party some supplies and rented them some boats and helped them establish the settlement they called Champ d'Aisle on the Trinity River near the present city of Liberty. The Spanish immediately heard about it, probably from Jean Laffite. A Spanish task force left San Antonio for the Trinity. The French heard about this and scattered. Joseph Bonaparte lost his chance to be king of Mexico.

The Laffites may also have tipped the Spanish that James Long was lurking around Galveston Bay. Long was a former U.S. Army surgeon from Virginia. Some people in Mississippi had raised a little volunteer army and put Dr. Long in charge of it. They wanted him to take Texas away from Spain. Long came here to ask the Laffites to help him. They declined. Long established a camp on Boliver Point. He called it Fort Las Casas. Mrs. Long and their daughter and a servant woman stayed at this crude settlement when Long sailed off with fifty-two of his followers in October, 1821, to try to capture the Spanish presidio at Goliad. The Spanish captured them. Dr. Long went to Mexico City as a prisoner. He was shot to death there by a prison guard in what was said to have been an accident.

Jane Long survived a hard winter on Bolivar Point and gave birth to another child there in December. Friends rescued her in July, 1822, and she went home to Mississippi. She returned to Texas in 1824 as one of Stephen F. Austin's colonists and lived in Texas until she died at Richmond in 1880.

The Laffites reportedly tried to keep the skippers of their privateers from stopping American ships. It was not out of sentiment. They just thought there was little future in it. Their colleagues stopped one or two American ships,

Jean Laffite had his headquarters in a big red house right on the water on the harbor side of the island. This house stood on the site until it fell down in the 1960s. This is not Laffite's "Maison Rouge." He burned all his buildings when he left. This house was built by another seafaring man years after Laffite left. The foundation is still standing. The property is owned by Douglas Zweiner of Houston. He says he has never found any artifacts except a few cannon balls. The site is on Water Street near the container dock.

anyway. A U.S. Navy warship sailed into the bay one day and served notice that the U.S. government wanted the privateers to leave. The Laffites agreed to go and negotiated a little time to get ready. What happened next has provided fuel for rumors of buried treasure ever since. Nobody knows that they did, but many people suppose that the Laffites had more booty on the island than they could carry away in the ships they had. Some people believe the pirates buried treasure in various places around the bay as far up as Clear Creek. The sites favored in most of the treasure legends are the place where Jean Laffite's house stood and the spot down the island known as Laffite's Grove or Three Trees. Some accounts say Laffite's privateers fought a battle with the Karankawa Indians at this little grove once. Other accounts say the privateers camped at the grove after a fight with the Indians. The one thing that seems certain is that the grove was the best landmark on the island. Most early accounts agree that there were no other trees here. The state put a stone marker in the grove in 1936. No one ever has reported finding any treasure in the grove, or in any of the other places the pirates supposedly buried booty. This does not necessarily mean no treasure was buried.

Six of Laffite's men stayed here when the pirate fleet left on March 3, 1821. James Campbell was one of them. Stephen Churchill was another. It is possible some of these men recovered some of the buried treasure. They would not necessarily have made an announcement about it. Not all of Laffite's men were privateers by design. Some of them were on ships the privateers captured. They simply joined the privateers as a matter of survival.

Jean Laffite set fire to his camp as he left. The buildings apparently all burned to the ground. Settlers arriving later in the 1820s reported lots of snakes, alligators and mosquitos but no buildings. The shape of the island was substantially different then. It is now a fairly solid piece of real estate about thirty miles long and varying up to about three miles in width. There are inlets and bayous and coves. One or more of these ran all the way through the island in Laffite's time. There was another channel into the harbor besides the one still in use. It ran through what is now the heart of the city. It filled in sometime before 1845, but the Sandusky map issued that year shows a bayou reaching in from the Gulf to Broadway. The island is made up of sand bars. They moved around before the seawall was built.

The history books mostly say the Laffites went from Galveston to somewhere in the southern Gulf of Mexico and eventually died or were killed near Yucatan. There is another story that Jean Laffite spread false rumors about his death and then settled in the United States. He married a woman named Emma Mortimer in this version and changed his name to Jean Lafflin and went into the gunpowder business in St. Louis. A journal apparently written by Laffite supports this latter version. It is in the Sam Houston Regional Library in Liberty.

PART THREE

The Great Years 1821-1900

Galveston Island was quiet for a little while after the pirates left. There was a shipwreck off San Luis Pass in the summer of 1822. The schooner *Lively* broke up and sank with all her crew and cargo. The ship was one Stephen F. Austin had bought to carry supplies and immigrants to his new colony on the Brazos River. The *Lively* had landed eighteen colonists and some cargo at the mouth of the Brazos in 1821 and had gone back to New Orleans. She sailed for Texas again in June, 1822, on the voyage she never completed.

Stephen F. Austin's colony was four years old before Austin got his first look at Galveston Bay in 1825. He said it was the best natural harbor he had seen. The Mexicans had thrown off Spanish rule by this time and Austin was dealing with the new government of Mexico. He asked the Mexican government to let him add this part of the coast to his colony. The Mexicans always were leery of letting Anglos settle on the coast or close to the U.S. border. The Mexicans did make Galveston a provisional port and they built a customs house.

Michel B. Menard resorted to subterfuge in making his first claim for land on the island. The Mexican government allowed native citizens to claim land just about anywhere they wanted if they had performed useful services for their country. Juan Seguin of San Antonio qualified. Menard persuaded him to claim the east end of Galveston Island as his headright in 1833. Menard then bought that claim from Seguin in 1834. It is estimated there were about 500 people living on the island at the time. Some of them almost

Michel B. Menard was born in Canada. He was an Indian trader as a young man. He settled in Texas in 1832. Menard was one of the signers of the Texas Declaration of Independence. He founded the city of Galveston on land he bought twice. Menard bought a claim from a Mexican citizen during colonial days and then bought the same land again from the Republic of Texas after the Battle of San Jacinto.

certainly were living on the land Menard claimed.

Ships continued to have trouble navigating along the coast. A ship carrying immigrants from Germany came to grief on a sand bar here in December, 1834. Some of the immigrants survived and waded ashore. Robert and Rosa Kleberg were among the survivors. Robert walked to Stephen F. Austin's headquarters at San Felipe to arrange a land grant. Robert and Rosa settled at Cat Spring. One of the sons they raised there married Richard King's daughter and became head of the King Ranch.

Texas colonists held a consultation at San Felipe in the fall of 1835 to talk about how unhappy they were with Mexican rule. They decided to stay with Mexico, but they determined to secede from Coahuila and make Texas a separate state. They established a provisional government. It purported to be a state government with Henry Smith as governor. States do not normally operate navies, but this one did. The provisional government bought four ships and also issued letters of marque to several privateers. This first

Opposite left: *David Burnet was president of the interim government of Texas during the revolution of 1836. He and most of his cabinet were in Galveston when they learned that Sam Houston had defeated Santa Anna at San Jacinto. Burnet lived in Galveston during his last years. He was buried here when he died in 1870, but his remains later were moved to the State Cemetery in Austin.*

Opposite right: *Gail Borden was a pioneer surveyor and publisher before he discovered how to condense milk. He first landed in Galveston in 1829 on his way to Stephen F. Austin's colonial headquarters at San Felipe. Borden came back to Galveston in 1837 as the first customs collector for the Republic of Texas. Gail Borden had a home on Avenue P until he moved to New York in 1851. He had an inventive mind. One of his inventions while he was here was a terraqueous machine. It was a wagon with a sail and he actually sailed it on the Galveston beach.*

Texas Navy was based on Galveston Island at Fort Point, about where the Coast Guard station is today, from 1835 until the last ship was lost in 1837.

There was some shooting at Gonzales and rebellious Texans had seized the Alamo by the end of 1835. The Convention of 1836 at Washington-on-the-Brazos that spring turned the rebellion into a war for independence. An interim government was established with David Burnet as president. The government officials fled to Harrisburg after Santa Anna recaptured the Alamo. Santa Anna headed for Harrisburg and almost caught them. Burnet and the other officers of the interim government hurried to New Washington on Morgan's Point and boarded the little sidewheel steamer *Cayuga*. The government leaders sailed to Galveston on the *Cayuga* on April 15, 1836. They stayed on board for ten days, ready to move again if necessary. They never dreamed that Sam Houston would catch the Mexicans off guard at San Jacinto. The word that Houston had destroyed the Mexican Army and captured Santa Anna reached Galveston on April 26. The sidewheeler *Yellowstone* was in Galveston harbor by this time. The interim government transferred to the *Yellowstone* and steamed up to San Jacinto on May 4 to celebrate the surprising victory.

The *Yellowstone* brought the Texas officials, Santa Anna and his staff and several dozen Mexican officers back to Galveston on May 9. Sam Houston had been wounded. He needed medical treatment. David Burnet was going to leave him on the battlefield, but the captain of the *Yellowstone* refused to leave San Jacinto without Houston. The general

SITE OF THE HOME
1837 - 1851, OF

GAIL BORDEN, JR.

PIONEER SURVEYOR, NEWSPAPER EDITOR
AND INVENTOR OF A PROCESS FOR CON-
DENSING MILK, WHICH HE DISCOVERED
WHILE LIVING HERE IN 1840 · · BORN
DECEMBER 5, 1801 · · DIED SEPTEMBER
2, 1874

was transferred here to the steamship *Flora* which took him to New Orleans with the Navy schooner *Liberty* as an escort. Houston had his wound tended and he recovered. The *Liberty* had some repairs made and the owners of the New Orleans shipyard seized her because the new republic could not pay the bill.

The Mexican officers the *Yellowstone* brought from San Jacinto were put ashore in Galveston. Colonel Pedro Delgado was one of them. He wrote an account of his experiences after he got back to Mexico. He said the Mexican officers were confined in an open camp commanded by Texas Colonel James Morgan. The colonel was the proprietor of the town of New Washington on Morgan's Point. He was the owner of Emily Morgan. She was the mulatto girl Santa Anna had with him in his tent at San Jacinto the afternoon of April 21 when he should have been paying more attention to what was going on outside. The Mexican colonel said Morgan was a hard man. Morgan had good reason; the Mexicans had burned his town. Delgado complained that the captured officers were exposed to the weather and mosquitos and sand crabs and a lot of abuse from Texans until the middle of August when they were transferred from Galveston to Hardin County. He said they were treated pretty well there until they were released in April, 1837.

Most historians say President Burnet and Santa Anna traveled from Galveston on the *Yellowstone* to Velasco. Delgado says Santa Anna was transferred at Galveston to the Texas warship *Independence*. He made it to Velasco, anyway. There he signed the treaties he thought would get him his freedom, but he was held prisoner for several months on the Phelps family plantation in Brazoria County before President Sam Houston sent him home by way of Washington.

The Texas Navy had three ships left after the *Liberty* was seized. Two of them went to New York for repairs. They were the *Brutus* and the *Invincible*. They would have been seized, too, but Sam Swartwout intervened and paid the bills. He had an ulterior motive. Swartwout was a big speculator in Texas land. He had some dubious claims he was trying to get validated. The Mexicans captured the schooner *Independence* off Velasco in April, 1837. The *Invincible* ran aground and broke up after engaging two Mexican warships off Galveston in August, 1837. The *Brutus* went down in a storm in the Gulf in October, 1837, and the republic was without a navy.

The Republic of Texas was born poor. Money was the most urgent need. The quickest practical way to get it was through customs duties. The republic established a customs office at Galveston and named Gail Borden the collector. He set up shop in the customs house the Mexicans had built. The Texas government built a new customs house, but it was swept away by a hurricane in the fall of 1837 before it was ever occupied. The same storm swept away the warehouse and dock Thomas McKinney and Samuel Williams had just built on the waterfront. McKinney and Williams had been in the import and export business at the mouth of the Brazos before the revolution. They moved their business to Galveston in 1837. They rebuilt the warehouse after the storm and built up a very large business. Borden did his customs business on board the brig *Perseverance* for nearly a year until his office was rebuilt.

The government established a fort at the eastern tip of the island. The guns came from the steamboat *Cayuga,* but it is not clear what happened to the steamboat itself. Michel B. Menard improved his claim to the east end of the island by buying a quit claim deed from the government of the Republic of Texas for $50,000. Menard had to borrow the money. The lender was soon selling shares in his interest.

One of Gail Borden's neighbors on Avenue P was Samuel May Williams. The Borden house is gone, but the Williams house still stands in the 3600 block. It is maintained by the Galveston Historical Foundation as a museum. Work started on the Williams house in 1838. It was completed in 1840.

McKinney, Williams and Borden joined Menard in forming the Galveston City Company. They agreed to issue 1,000 shares of stock at $1,000 each. They had to use some of the stock to settle with other claimants to the land. The stock did not sell well. The company took some of it back in exchange for lots. The value of the $1,000 shares actually sank to about $100 in the early 1840s.

There were seven houses in Galveston by the end of 1837, and traffic in the port was increasing. Commodore Charles Morgan started regular service between New Orleans and Galveston with the steamboat *Columbia*. His dock was about where Pier 21 is now. This service was the beginning of the Morgan Line.

The Galveston City Company started offering town lots for sale in 1838 and the republic started buying a new navy. The City Company had the townsite laid out in streets and avenues. The avenues were laid parallel to the waterfront and named for the letters of the alphabet. The intersecting streets were given numbers.The city developed from the channel side. The beach front development all came later. The more remote blocks were originally much larger than those close in. Those remote blocks were subdivided as the city grew. Additional avenues were laid out between the original avenues. The names of the original avenues were not changed. The new avenues were simply given names that made it perfectly clear where they were. Avenue O½ is the avenue between O and P and so on. The City Company donated lots for churches. Some people even got water frontage free by guaranteeing to build wharves and

warehouses to help get development started. The City Company sold 700 lots the first year at an average price of $400 a lot. One of the first buyers was Joseph Osterman from Holland. He bought a corner lot at Market and Tremont and built a store there.

The first ship in the second Texas Navy was the brig *Potomac*. She was docked at Fort Point and used as a receiving ship. The other ships the Navy acquired in 1838 and 1839 were the steampacket *Zavalla;*the schooners *San Jacinto*, *San Antonio* and *San Bernard;* the brigs *Wharton* and *Archer;* and the sloop *Austin*. President Mirabeau Lamar brought in a young U.S. Navy lieutenant named Edwin Moore to be commodore of this fleet. The *San Jacinto* was wrecked in 1840. President Lamar sided with Yucatan when that state rebelled against Mexico in 1841. Lamar rented the *Austin,* the *San Bernard,* the *San Antonio* and Commodore Moore to the rebels for $8,000 a month. Lamar's term ended in December, 1841, and he was succeeded by Sam Houston the same day the fleet sailed for Yucatan.

Opposite: *This home at 1605 33rd Street was built about the same time as the Williams house. It is not clear which is older, but they are the two oldest houses in Galveston. This was the home of the founder of the city. It has not been very well maintained and the present owner wants to sell it.*

Right: *The oldest surviving church building in Galveston is St. Mary's Cathedral. It was the first Roman Catholic Cathedral in Texas. Work started on St. Mary's at 21st Street and Church in 1847.*

Houston immediately cancelled the arrangement and ordered the fleet back home. The order did not reach the commodore until March. The skipper of the *San Antonio* received the president's order when he returned to Galveston in January to deliver some messages from the commodore. The *San Antonio* was a long time rejoining the fleet off Yucatan. She went by way of New Orleans to deliver some shipwreck survivors she had picked up. Part of the crew mutinied and killed one of the officers while the *San Antonio* was in New Orleans. The U.S. Navy intervened and captured the mutineers. Four mutineers were hanged. It was the only mutiny in the history of the Texas Navy. The *San Antonio* reached Yucatan in March. She and the other Texas ships returned to Galveston in May. The *San Antonio* went to Yucatan again in September to collect the rent and she disappeared. She was presumed lost in a storm. The steamboat *Zavalla* needed repairs the Navy could not afford. She was deliberately run aground at Galveston in 1842 and later broken up for scrap.

Commodore Moore took the rest of the fleet to New Orleans for refitting. He had to pay most of the bills himself because President Houston was withholding the appropriations Congress had approved for the work. Houston sent Moore orders to return to Galveston, but Moore made excuses. He was afraid Houston would sell the ships if he got them back in Texas waters. Houston never was the big army and navy booster that Lamar was. Houston sent three naval commissioners to New Orleans to make the commodore obey his orders. One of the commissioners was the Galveston businessman Samuel Williams. Another one was the former Galveston prisoner-of-war camp commandant, James Morgan. Commodore Moore persuaded the commissioners to let him take the fleet to sea to see if he could find some action. Colonel Morgan went with him. They took the *Austin* and the *Wharton* down to the coast of Yucatan. They tangled with Mexican warships three times between the end of April and the middle of May, 1843.

President Houston was so provoked by this insubordination that he issued a public notice branding Moore and his men as pirates and inviting any friendly government to capture them and send them home. Commodore Moore sailed for Galveston as soon as he heard about this. The *Handbook of Texas* says Moore got a hero's welcome from the citizens when he reached here July 14, but President Houston fired him. The commodore appealed to Congress and got a court-martial to hear his case. The court decided he had done nothing wrong, but he did not get his job back. Houston got Congress to authorize him to sell the fleet at a public auction. The people of Galveston disrupted the bidding and the sale had to be cancelled. But the ships did not sail again. They were laid up in Galveston until Texas was annexed to the United States. The four surviving ships were transferred to the U.S. Navy in June, 1846, and the Texas Navy expired. The U.S. Navy immediately scrapped three of the Texas ships. The *Austin* was used as a receiving ship at Pensacola for a while and then she was scrapped.

Galveston County was organized in 1838 with Galveston as the county seat. Work started in 1838 on two substan-

Left: *The oldest religious congregation in Galveston is the First Presbyterian. The congregation built this church in 1845 at the corner of 19th and Church Street. It no longer stands.*

Below: *The present First Presbyterian Church, on the opposite side of Church Street, was built in 1873.*

Left: *The First Baptist Church of Galveston occupies a half block on Sealy between 22nd and 23rd streets. The congregation is one of the oldest, but this building was built in 1958. It is the fourth building the First Baptist Church has occupied. The earlier buildings faced 22nd Street. This building faces 23rd Street on the site occupied earlier by the home of the late John Sealy.*

Opposite top: *The First Methodist Church was established in 1840 on this site at 22nd and Church streets. The building occupying the site now is the Scottish Rite Cathedral. The Scottish Rite lodge here was the first in Texas. It was founded in 1867. This building was built in 1929.*

tial homes that still stand. Most of the materials for the Michel B. Menard house at 1603 33rd Street and the Samuel Williams house at 3601 Avenue P were shipped from New England.

Hamilton Stuart started publishing the *Civilian and Galveston Gazette* in 1838. Stuart actually had started publishing the paper in Houston a little earlier the same year. He had the backing of Dr. Levi Jones when he moved the paper here. Jones was one of the charter members of the Galveston City Company. Stuart was from Kentucky.

There was a little settlement in San Luis Pass off the west end of Galveston Island by 1838. Most of the transportation then was by water.There was substantial traffic between Galveston and the mouth of the Brazos. San Luis Island probably seemed a logical spot for a settlement, but it was not a very practical one. San Luis had the first cotton press in Texas in 1839, but everybody moved away soon after that because the site was so low every high tide flooded the town. It was just a sand bar off what was then usually

called the Velasco Peninsula.

Galveston was growing fast. The city was incorporated in 1839 and divided into three wards. The original arrangement called for a mayor and four aldermen from each of the three wards. John M. Allen was the first mayor. He was from Kentucky and a veteran of San Jacinto. The population was about 1,000. There were 250 houses, two wharves, two hotels, several warehouses, a customs house and a post office. The original Galveston post office was a frame shack on The Strand at 23rd Street. P.J. Menard was the first postmaster. There sometimes were as many as thirty ships in the harbor. Three steamers made regular trips to Houston. Most of the trade was with U.S. ports. The first cargo to go directly from Galveston to England left here in 1839 in the English bark *Ambassador*. A cargo went directly to France the next year in the *Fils Unique*. The cargoes were cotton.

One of the two wharves in use in 1838 was Kuhn's at 18th Street. Ephraim McLean built it. He was from

Left: *Trinity Episcopal Church at 22nd Street and Winnie was built in 1857 by the Episcopalian congregation the Reverend Benjamin Eaton organized here in 1841.*

67

Left: *Some of Galveston's leading citizens were Episcopalians. John Sealy, John Henry Hutchings, T.M. League and Henry Rosenberg were members of Trinity Episcopal. Henry Rosenberg paid half the cost when the church built the Eaton Chapel at 22nd Street and Ball in 1877.*

Below: *The B'nai Israel Synagogue was considerably more distinguished when it was built in 1870 on 22nd Street between Ball and Sealy. The building originally had four minarets. The center section where the two rows of small windows are now was originally a large stained glass window. The congregation sold the building and moved to a new location in 1953.*

St. Patrick's Catholic Church was designed by Nicholas Clayton and completed in 1878. The building at 3420 Avenue K was badly damaged by the 1900 storm. It was rebuilt and then jacked up five feet when the elevation of the city was raised.

Kentucky and he came here first as skipper of the *Columbus*. The other wharf was built by McKinney and Williams at 24th Street to replace the dock they lost in the hurricane in 1837. McKinney and Williams had almost finished building a hotel when that storm hit. Their uncompleted Tremont Hotel was demolished; so they started work on a new and bigger Tremont at 23rd and Church streets. The new Tremont Hotel opened on San Jacinto Day in 1839 and for years after that it was the finest hotel in Texas.

A.C. Crawford and a few friends organized the first Galveston fire company in 1839. It was called The Bucket Company. The name was later changed to Hook and Ladder Company Number One. Firefighting was an upper-class exercise in the beginning.

Galveston's first yellow fever epidemic in 1839 claimed 250 lives. One of the few doctors here then was Ashbel Smith. Some of the doctors practicing in Texas in the early days were self-taught. Ashbel Smith was not one of those. He had a medical degree from Yale and he had studied in France before he came to Texas in 1837.

Galveston was clearly the principal city in Texas in 1840 with a population of about 3,000. The Congress of the Republic issued Galveston a new charter in 1840. It specified that only property owners could vote in city elections. A new election was held in June and John Walton was elected mayor. John Allen had just been reelected under the old charter. Both men claimed the office until August when the district court ruled that Walton was the legally elected mayor.

Top left: *German Catholics built St. Joseph's Church on Avenue K at 22nd Street in 1859. The German Catholics were assimilated into the other parishes a long time ago. The church building is maintained now by the Galveston Historical Foundation as a museum and meeting house.*

Bottom: *The oldest black Baptist church on the island is the Avenue L Baptist Church on Avenue L at 26th Street. Members of the First Baptist Church organized this church for their slaves in 1847. It was originally called the Colored Baptist Church. The name was changed to African Baptist Church after the Civil War. The present building was completed in 1916.*

Opposite left: *The First Lutheran Church was established in 1844. The present building at 24th Street and Winnie was built in 1850 and rebuilt in 1915.*

Opposite right: *The oldest black Methodist church in Galveston is Reedy Chapel at 2013 Broadway. White Methodists bought this lot in 1848 as a place of worship for their slaves. The first building was built in 1863. It was named the African Methodist Church after the Civil War. The building was destroyed by the great fire of 1885. This building was built in 1887. It had to be rebuilt after the 1900 storm and it has been remodeled twice since then. It is called Reedy Chapel in honor of the late Reverend Houston Reedy. He was the first pastor.*

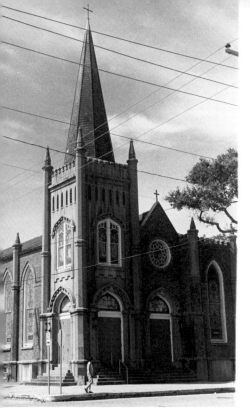

The organization of churches began in 1840. The Reverend John McCullough came from Pennsylvania to organize the first Presbyterian congregation on January 1. The first Baptist congregation was organized January 30 in the home of Gail Borden's brother, Tom. Both the Bordens and their wives were charter members. The original Baptist minister here was the Reverend James Huckins from New Hampshire. The first Methodist congregation was organized the same year with the Reverend Thomas O. Summers as pastor. The first religious services in Galveston surely were Roman Catholic. No other services were legal in Texas before the revolution. The first Catholic priest stationed here was Father John Odin from France. Galveston became a prefecture in 1840, a vicariate in 1842 and a diocese in 1847 with Odin as bishop. The original Galveston diocese included all of Texas.

Samuel Bangs was back in Galveston by 1840. He came first with Francisco Mina in 1816 when Mina was organizing his attempt to invade Mexico. Bangs printed Mina's

Top: *Many of the houses built in Galveston before the Civil War were in the style the architects call Greek Revival. This one was more than a house. John Sydnor built it as a family hotel in 1848. He called it Powhatan House. It was not very successful. The building was later divided. This section at 3427 Avenue O is now the headquarters of the Galveston Garden Club.*

Bottom: *The raised cottage now standing at 1721 Broadway was built in 1850 at the corner of Broadway and 14th Street. The Walter Greshams had this house moved here in 1886 because they wanted the original site for the stone mansion now known as the Bishop's Palace. This house was the home of a lawyer named J.Z.H. Scott. It was a ruin until the Lee Trenthams restored it in 1981. It is now a doll museum.*

Opposite: *Banker George Ball built a Greek Revival mansion at 23rd Street and Sealy in 1857. The Rosenberg Library stands on the site now. The library was built in 1902 after the Ball house was divided into two houses and moved to the 1400 block of 24th Street. This is part of the original Ball house. The other half is next door.*

orders and pamphlets. The Spanish took him prisoner when they captured Mina, but they treated him better than they did Mina. Bangs lived in Mexico for a while. He was back in Texas by 1839. He came back to Galveston after he failed to get a job with the *Telegraph and Texas Register* in Houston. He started at least three papers in Galveston. They were the *Galvestonian,* the *Chronicle* and the *Globe.* Some accounts say he also started the *Galveston News* and sold it to Wilbur Cherry and Michael Cronican. Other accounts say Cherry and Cronican started the *Galveston News* with a press Bangs had used earlier.

John S. Sydnor moved his family from Virginia to Galveston in 1840. He started a farm and a dairy because he could see that the growing city was going to need more food. Sydnor quickly moved on into more lucrative endeavors, but there were many farms and ranches on the island in the early days. Visitors in the 1840s often remarked upon the quantity and quality of the fresh produce available.

The first cotton compress was installed in Galveston in 1840. It was a small steam hydraulic press imported from England and it evidently did not work very well. It was used for only one season, but there were several other presses established in the city shortly afterward. Some were steam and hydraulic and some were wood screw presses using horse or ox power. Cotton was being sent out from the plantations in those days in very loose bales weighing about 500 pounds each. Anything the cotton merchants in Galveston could do to reduce the size of the bales was money in the bank because it meant they could fit more bales into a ship.

Top: *The Jesuits established the University of St. Mary in 1854. The university building was at 13th Street and Avenue I (Sealy). It and the Jesuits' Sacred Heart Church occupied the entire block from Sealy to Broadway, from 13th to 14th by the time the 1900 storm struck. The hurricane damaged the university and demolished the church. The church was rebuilt. The Sacred Heart Convent and School now occupy the site where the university was.*

Right: *Galveston was the most important trading and banking center in Texas by the 1850s. One of the most successful early settlers was John Henry Hutchings. He came to Galveston in the 1840s. and joined another newcomer named John Sealy. They moved to Sabine and opened a store. Sealy and Hutchings returned to Galveston in 1854 and joined George Ball in a commission and banking concern that made them all rich. Hutchings built a mansion at 2816 Avenue O in 1859. It is still in the Hutchings family.*

Bottom: *Henry Rosenberg came to Galveston from Switzerland in 1843. He started working as a clerk in a dry goods company.*

74

The size of the bales was reduced by about half even with the primitive early presses. A lot of energy and ingenuity went into improving the cotton presses.

The first Episcopal parish was organized in 1841 after the Reverend Benjamin Eaton arrived from Ireland. It was Trinity parish. The first services were held in the courthouse. The population of the city by this time was very cosmopolitan. There were people from England, Germany, Holland, Italy, the United States and Mexico. Many of them were well educated and cultured. Galveston was more aware of the rest of the world than most of Texas would be years later. A German newspaper called the *Galveston Zeitung* started publishing here in 1841 and continued until 1855. The first reserve military organization in Texas was established here in 1841. It was the Galveston Artillery. It survives today as a private club.

The pioneer merchant Joseph Osterman brought some oleander cuttings to Galveston in 1841. His sister planted them in her yard at 25th Street and Avenue I where the Southern Union Gas Company is now. The historical marker at this site says these were the first oleanders here. There is another story. It holds that the first oleanders were brought here years earlier by a Norwegian. He had some plants with him when the ship he was on was captured by Laffite's pirates. He supposedly planted them here and the pirates called them oleanders because his name was Ole Anderson. The first plants came from the Caribbean in both versions. They originally came from the Mediterranean.

A hurricane swept over the island in 1841. There was another one in 1842. An English writer named William Bollaert spent a good bit of time here in 1842. He wrote about the storm and he also complained that, when he was lying in his bed at night under the mosquito bar, the mosquitos made so much noise he could not sleep. There were no window screens then. Every bed had a net canopy called a mosquito bar. Bollaert was staying at the Tremont. He thought the people he met in Galveston were living pretty well and he wrote approvingly of the leisurely meals he had on the Tremont veranda.

The first issue of the *Galveston News* came out on April 11, 1842. Galveston has had at least three dozen newspapers over the years. There were three or four before the *News*, but they did not last. The *Galveston News* did. It is the oldest newspaper in Texas.

J.W. Branham was mayor in 1842. This was the year Thomas Jefferson League came to Galveston with his parents. Thomas was eight years old. His brother, John Charles League, was born here. They both became prominent businessmen. League City was named for this family. The Trinity Episcopal parish built its first small church at Winnie and Tremont in 1842.

John M. Allen was back in the mayor's office in 1843. Henry Rosenberg came from Switzerland and went to work for dry goods merchant John Hessly. Rosenberg would become one of Galveston's most important citizens. Wilbur Cherry of the *Galveston News* took in a partner named B. F. Neal and they hired Willard Richardson to edit the paper. This was probably the most important event in the history of the *Galveston News*.

Willard Richardson was born in Massachusetts, but he got most of his education in South Carolina. He came to Texas in 1837. He worked as a surveyor and did some teaching before he was hired to edit the *Telegraph and Texas Register* in Houston. His work in Houston attracted the attention of Cherry and Neal. Richardson bought out Cherry and Neal in 1845 and plunged into advocacy journalism. He was a disciple of John C. Calhoun. He was for slavery and against Sam Houston. He was opposed to almost everything

Opposite: *Henry Rosenberg was one of the richest and most influential men in Galveston by the time he built this home at 1306 Market in 1859. He had no children. He left most of his fortune for the benefit of his fellow Galvestonians. The Rosenberg home is now divided into small apartments.*

Above: *Another example of Galveston's restrained antebellum architecture is the Poole Parker house at 3419 Avenue L. This house was built about 1860.*

Hamilton Stuart of the *Civilian* was for. Galveston newspaper readers were exposed to some lively writing for the next thirty years.

William and Joseph Hendley came from Connecticut in 1845 to start William Hendley and Company on The Strand. Work started on the First Presbyterian Church building at 19th and Church streets. Galvestonians had started modifying the original alphabetical and numerical street system. Avenue F became Church Street because some of the earliest churches were on it, but it is also still known as Avenue F. Avenue A became Front Street and then Water Street. Avenue B is almost always called The Strand. Avenue C is also Mechanic Street. Avenue D is also Market Street. Avenue E is also Postoffice Street. This is because the first U.S. Post Office was built on this street, but the street got most of its fame from another kind of activity.

That first U.S. Post Office was not built on Avenue E until later, but the United States took over the postal service in Texas at the end of 1845. The Texas Congress

James M. Brown built this house for his family in 1859. Brown called it Ashton Villa. Ashton was Mrs. Brown's maiden name. This was the most ostentatious house in Galveston until well after the Civil War. This house came close to being demolished in the 1970s, but it was saved and restored. The Galveston Historical Foundation maintains it now as a museum.

approved annexation in June. A special convention ratified the decision on July 4. The annexation took effect December 29. Texas was the biggest state in the Union. Galveston was the biggest city in Texas. The population was about 3,500.

John Sealy arrived from Pennsylvania in 1846. John S. Sydnor was elected mayor of Galveston in 1846. He established the first public school. Sydnor got the legislature to authorize the city to levy a school tax. His administration collected the tax, rented a building, hired some teachers, and started educating children. Historian Charles Hayes says subsequent administrations found it inconvenient to continue levying the tax; so the school closed. It was a long time before Galveston had a public school again, but it was not long before the city had another school.

A party of Ursuline nuns arrived from New Orleans in 1847 to establish the Ursuline Academy. Work also started in 1847 on St. Mary's Catholic Cathedral at 2011 Church Street. Relatives of Father J.M. Pacquin donated half a million bricks for the church and had them shipped from

Belgium to Galveston as a memorial to Pacquin. The priest had died in Galveston of yellow fever he contracted while working among fever victims during the city's second fever epidemic in 1844. Four hundred others died during that epidemic.

Texans were suspicious of banks and bankers in the early days. There was no provision for banks in the constitution of the Republic or in the original state constitution. But Samuel May Williams established the Commercial and Agricultural Bank in Galveston in 1847. He claimed it was legal because he had a charter the Mexican government issued him before the revolution.

Mayor Sydnor started work in 1847 on the city's first family hotel at 21st Street and Avenue M. He called it Powhatan House. It was not a big success. The building was later divided up and moved. Part of it now stands at 3427 Avenue O on a site that was originally part of the Borden estate. Members of the First Baptist Church organized a church for their slaves in 1847. It was originally called the Colored Baptist Church. White Methodists bought a lot at 2013 Broadway for a place of worship for their slaves. It was originally called the African Methodist Church. Norris Wright Cuney was a member of this church.

Joseph Bates succeeded John Sydnor as mayor in 1848. The Union Marine and Fire Insurance Company was chartered that year with Albert Ball as president.

The *Civilian* editor, Hamilton Stuart, was elected mayor in 1849. The R.&D.G. Mills Company moved to Galveston that year from Brazoria County. The Mills brothers were cotton brokers and merchants.They had come from Kentucky in 1830 and they had made a lot of money before they moved here. Robert Mills was often called the Duke of Brazoria because he owned four plantations and more than 800 slaves. Robert's brother, David, actually tended to the plantation end of their business. Robert concerned himself mostly with buying and selling cotton and running their big unofficial banking business.

The first official U.S. census in Texas in 1850 confirmed Galveston's position as the biggest city in the state. The

Top: *Galveston was the first city
in Texas to have gas lights and
gas heat. Southern Union Gas
Company now operates the
system that started on this site
in 1859. The original Galveston
Gas and Coke Company made its
gas from coal imported from
England. The company had four
customers in 1859.*

Bottom: *Galveston was a city of
beautiful homes and
distinguished public buildings at
the beginning of the Civil War.
The county government and the
district court were quartered in
this building, built in 1856. The
building in the background at the
left housed the court of appeals.*

Most of the mail for Texas came in through Galveston. It was natural that the first U.S. government building to be started in Texas after annexation was the Galveston post office. It was finished just in time to be taken over by the Confederacy in 1861. This was also the federal court building until 1891.

population was 4,177. The richest man in town was R.S. Rose. He was a land speculator worth about $110,000. Shiploads of German immigrants were coming in by this time. Many of them went on to the Hill Country to settle. Some of them settled on the island. The population of Galveston was almost half German by the middle 1850s. Shipowners in Europe were encouraging migrants to make Galveston their destination so their ships could load up with Texas cotton for the trip back. The population of Galveston and Texas was increasing rapidly. The economy was expanding in a pattern that encouraged Texans to cling to the doomed institution of slavery.

The Congress of the United States had banned the importation of slaves from Africa in 1808. The Mexican government had laws against bringing in slaves from anywhere. The Republic of Texas allowed and encouraged slavery, but the laws then, too, prohibited importation of slaves from Africa. There had never been a time since the Anglo settlement began when it was legal to bring in slaves from Africa.

One of the most important commercial blocks in Galveston at the time of the Civil War was the 2000 block of The Strand. The Hendley Buildings here were occupied by retailers and cotton brokers. There are four identical buildings in a row. The one with the flags is now the headquarters of the Galveston Historical Foundation. The Hendley Buildings were hit by cannon balls several times during the Battle of Galveston on New Year's Day in 1863.

But there was some smuggling from the beginning. It was increasing in the 1850s.

Texans thought there was no limit to the demand for Texas cotton and they thought there was no limit to the amount they could produce if they had enough labor. Many planters and businessmen and some journalists and politicians convinced themselves that whatever it took to produce more cotton would be justified. The number of slaves in Texas increased from 58,000 to 182,000 during the 1850s. Most of the slaves were brought in from the Old South, where some plantations were making a business of raising slaves. Thousands more were smuggled in from Africa by British and American slave traders and many of them were landed on the beaches around Galveston.

The demand for slaves was such that free Negroes sometimes were seized and sold into slavery. There were not many free Negroes in Texas in the 1850s, but free Negro seamen sometimes came into Galveston on foreign merchant ships. British Consul Arthur Lynn complained more than once about British Negro seamen being kidnapped in Galveston. The consul on one occasion engineered the recapture of a kidnapped seaman.

Reasonably reputable citizens hatched several plans to install a puppet government in Nicaragua so that nation could be a staging area for the slave trade. Others lobbied to get the laws changed. Hamilton Stuart of the *Civilian* and Willard Richardson of the *News* both favored almost any measure that would get more slave labor for Texas planters. Stuart changed his mind before 1861. Richardson never did. The end justified any means in Richardson's view. He wrote in the *News* that Texas cotton production could be increased from 300,000 bales a year to 7,000,000 bales if only there were enough slaves. He said Texans had a duty to develop the state's resources.

Slavers could land slaves on the Texas coast in the 1850s for a total cost of about $110 each. That included the bribes they expected to have to pay the British ships patrolling the African coast. The slaves could be sold in Texas for $1,000

Sam Houston was governor of Texas when Texans decided to secede from the United States. Houston did all he could to prevent secession. The Secession Convention removed him from the governor's office. Houston came to Galveston to make a speech from the balcony of the Tremont Hotel to warn that secession would bring on a war the South almost certainly would lose. Galvestonians listened, but they were not convinced.

to $1,200 each. Authorities were saying the same thing other authorities would say later about the rumrunning: there was just no way to prevent people from doing something that paid that much.

Smuggling slaves was profitable and some people claimed it was necessary, but slave smugglers were not socially acceptable. Slave dealers were. The big ones in Galveston during this time were C.L. McCarthy and John S. Sydnor. Former mayor Sydnor had a big voice and he did his own auctioneering. Most of the slaves in Galveston were house servants. Some were craftsmen. Some accounts say the reputable slave dealers made it their business when owners died to see that loyal and valuable city slaves were not shipped off to plantations where they might become field hands.

Much of the mail for points west of Galveston came here from New Orleans by ship in the 1850s. Contractors carried it on to Velasco and Victoria by stage and ferry. One of the contractors was Julius Lobenstein. He had his stables at 20th Street and Winnie. People in the interior complained sometimes that the Eastern newspapers were held up in Galveston until the Galveston papers could copy all the news.

The principal schools in the 1850s were operated by the Catholics. Girls of all faiths attended the Ursuline Academy and boys did not have to be Catholic to attend the school the Oblates of Mary Immaculate maintained. The legislature appropriated a little money for public education in the early 1850s. Galveston's share was used to pay tuition in the private schools for a few children from poor families.

Gail Borden perfected a dried meat biscuit about this time. He thought it was just what people needed to carry with them when they were traveling. The biscuit won a grand prize at the London Exhibition in 1851. Borden moved to New York to try to turn it into a business. The biscuit never caught on, but the formula he perfected for condensing milk in 1856 did catch on. It was the beginning of the Borden Company.

The German Lutheran Church was established in 1850. This is the church now called First Evangelical Lutheran.

Lorenzo Sherwood built a big home at 15th Street and Market. He was a lawyer from New York. He had been in Galveston only four years, but he would be representing Galveston in the Texas legislature a few years later.

Galveston had about fifty lawyers in the 1850s and about an equal number of doctors. The late Earl Fornell said in *The Galveston Era* that there were two upper classes in Galveston by this time. The Anglo professionals and business leaders made up one and the prosperous Germans made up the other. The working class was a mixture of Anglos, Germans and Mexicans. Leaders in business and the professions usually held the elective offices, with the support of the working classes. All white males over twenty-one were eligible to vote if they had been in Galveston for a year and had paid their taxes. Taxes were low. Most of the cost of public institutions was paid by the shippers and traders in the form of fees and licenses.

German immigrant Michael Seeligson was mayor in 1852 when the U.S. Congress authorized the first official survey

The Union fleet blockaded Galveston throughout the Civil War and Union troops occupied the city for about three months. Confederate forces led by General John Bankhead Magruder took the city back on January 1, 1863. The Southerners captured the Union warship Harriet Lane *and converted her to a blockade runner. The* Harriet Lane's *bell was displayed in Sam Houston Park in Houston for a long time. It is now on display in the museum on board the Battleship* Texas *at the San Jacinto Battleground.*

85

Confederate General John Magruder was a Virginian. Texans adopted him after he evicted the Union forces from Galveston in 1863. Magruder was buried in Houston when he died there in 1871. Confederate veterans moved his remains to the old City Cemetery here and put up this monument to the hero of the Battle of Galveston.

of harbors on the Texas coast. The surveyors concluded that the harbor at Galveston was the most promising, but there had been some shoaling. The water was just five feet deep at the inner bar.

Galveston News editor, Willard Richardson, was mayor in 1853 when the Galveston, Houston and Henderson Railroad was chartered. James Cronican was mayor in 1854 when the first telegraph line was completed from Galveston to Houston. The University of St. Mary was established at Avenue I and 13th Street in 1854.

The wharves and waterfront warehouses in Galveston were operated by assorted individuals and companies until 1854. Michel B. Menard, Samuel M. Williams, John Sealy, Henry Rosenberg and a few associates bought most of the wharves and organized the Galveston Wharf and Cotton Press Company on February 4 of that year. John Sealy and John Hutchings started a commission and banking business with George Ball.

Captain J.E. Haviland was mayor of Galveston in 1855

The first black Texan to gain political clout was Norris Wright Cuney. He was born in Waller County, went to school in Pennsylvania and settled here after the Civil War. Cuney got into politics during the Republican carpetbag period and controlled the Republican Party in Texas during most of the 1880s and 1890s. He also owned a stevedoring company.

when work began on the Galveston, Houston and Henderson rail line to Houston. The Reverend Benjamin Eaton laid the cornerstone for a new Trinity Episcopal Church building. The first Jewish religious services on the island were held in 1856 in the home of Isidore Dyer. The congregation that grew from this beginning became B'nai Israel in 1868.

Michel B. Menard died in 1856. John Sealy succeeded Menard as head of the Wharf Company and his relatives headed the company until after the city bought the private interests out in the 1940s. The county built a new courthouse in 1856. T.H. Brown was mayor.

The pattern that railroad development was taking caused serious concern in Galveston in the 1850s. The emphasis was upon lines crossing the country from east to west. It was plain to Galvestonians this would be more helpful to Houston than to Galveston. Galveston leaders tried to promote the idea of a rail system fanning out from Galveston into the interior. One of the more eloquent proponents of this system was the lawyer Lorenzo Sherwood. Willard

Richardson and the *News* supported him. Sherwood was elected to the legislature. He argued there for the Galveston railroad plan and for having the state itself build the railroads instead of giving big subsidies and land grants to private promoters. Richardson and the *News* went along and Sherwood eventually had Governor E.M. Pease thinking his way. Some of Galveston's entrepreneurs were shocked. They did not want the state building railroads. They began to accuse the New Yorker of being a socialist. They also said he was a Yankee abolitionist opposed to the "divine institution of slavery." A group of prominent Galvestonians led by Samuel Williams forced Sherwood to resign from the legislature. They may have used threats of violence. They also prevented Sherwood from appearing at a public meeting where he had planned to explain his position on slavery and railroads. Sherwood put his defense in writing. Hamilton Stuart of the *Civilian* published it for him. Willard Richardson of the *News* had shifted to the prevailing side. Richardson made no objection when the legislature rejected the Galveston plan and decided to encourage private railroad promoters with subsidies and land grants.

Galveston got a third strong newspaper in 1857 when Ferdinand Flake bought the *Weekly Union*. The paper had been started two years earlier by another German named Muhr. Flake had been in Texas since 1840. He was in the grocery and cigar business before he bought the paper he called *Die Union*. Secession fever was rising in Texas. Most of the immigrants from Germany were opposed to it. Ferdinand Flake spoke their sentiments. He often sided with the Republicans. Willard Richardson of the *News* was a deep-dyed slavery and secession Democrat. Hamilton Stuart of the *Civilian* was a Democrat, too, but he was becoming a strong Unionist.

The *Galveston News* was the most influential newspaper in the state. Richardson used the paper to help defeat Sam Houston's bid for the governor's office in 1857. Houston was in the U.S. Senate at the time. He was a slave owner, but he was strongly opposed to secession and in favor of preserving the Union. His views were contrary to those held by most members of the Texas legislature.

Houston knew he was not going to be named to another term in the Senate. The *Galveston News* attacked Houston's record all the way back to San Jacinto. Richardson told his readers Houston never was a great general. He said the idea that he was was only a myth. Houston came to Galveston on May 18 and rented the Morian Hall for a speech denouncing Richardson and the *News*. Houston drew a crowd, but most Galvestonians and most Texans voted that fall for Hardin Runnels for governor. Houston still had his seat in the Senate. His term was not up until 1859. He was soon planning to run for governor again.

Galveston had an estimated 7,000 residents by 1857. Some stylish buildings were going up. Trinity Church was completed and banker George Ball built a stately home at 23rd Street and Avenue I. Visitors exclaimed over the fine gardens and the great comforts available to the rich in Galveston. The *Galveston News* printed the first *Texas Almanac* in 1857. The steamship *Louisiana* caught fire on

Galveston's economy recovered quickly when the Civil War ended. W.L. Moody was one of the people attracted to the booming port city. Moody came to Texas from Virginia. He was a lawyer and merchant in Fairfield before the Civil War. He started brokering cotton here and put the Moody family on the way to becoming the richest on the island.

a trip from Indianola and sank off Galveston beach on May 31. Thirty-five people died. Galvestonians were so affected by the sight of the victims' bodies washing ashore that they organized a lifeboat company to rescue the victims of shipwrecks.

Samuel May Williams died in 1858. His partner, Thomas McKinney, had moved to Travis County five years before. Hutchings, Sealy and Company absorbed the Williams and McKinney wharf and banking interests. T.M. Joseph was mayor.

Two brothers from France moved to Galveston in 1858 and opened a store that evolved later into the Leon and H. Blum wholesale house.

William Hendley and Company built the Hendley buildings on The Strand with materials imported from the East Coast. The U.S. Post Office Department started work in 1858 on a post office building on Avenue E. It was the first U.S. government building built in Texas. There were several foundries and sailmakers on the waterfront by this time. The port was handling about 200,000 bales of cotton per season.

The Galveston, Houston and Henderson rail line was finished between Houston and Virginia Point, on the mainland opposite the island. A steam ferry boat carried passengers between Virginia Point and Galveston. Galvestonians approved a bond issue to pay for a bridge across the bay and trains were running into Galveston by 1860.

Work started in 1859 on St. Joseph's German Catholic Church at 2206 Avenue K and on several large homes. The earlier homes on the island had been frame. The Henry Rosenberg home at 1306 Market, the Walter Grover house between 15th and 16th streets on Market and the J.M. Brown house on Broadway were built of stone and brick. The Brown house may have been the first brick house in Texas. J.M. Brown worked as a brick mason before he came to Galveston and got rich in the hardware business. There was no brickyard here when he got ready to build. So he built a brickyard to make the bricks. Most of the construction was done by slaves. Brown was president of the new

Galveston, Houston and Henderson Railroad. He was one of the organizers of the new Galveston Gas and Coke Company. He was also one of the first customers when the company started making gas from imported English coal in 1859. His house had gas chandeliers and gas fireplaces. It was the first house in Galveston to have water piped indoors.

Work started in 1859 on the John Henry Hutchings house at 2816 Avenue O. Galveston was the banking center of Texas and Hutchings was one of the leading bankers. Banks still were not legal in Texas and the state had taken Samuel May Willams to court to try to make him stop representing himself as a banker. The biggest banking concern in Texas in the 1850s was the R.&D.G. Mills Company of Galveston. The Mills brothers and Williams got into banking the same way. They were cotton factors. They bought cotton from planters and sold it to mills in Europe and the eastern U.S. The transactions usually were not for cash. The factors would give the planters notes. The planters could exchange the notes for whatever they needed. Merchants accepted this paper at full face value. It was money in everything but name.

Sam Houston was elected governor in 1859. He was still a Unionist. Sentiment in Texas was increasingly for secession, but Houston got almost 9,000 votes more than the slave owners' friend, Hardin Runnels. Galveston did not go for Houston. The vote here was 403 for Runnels and 307 for Houston. The legislature elected to the United States Senate Houston's old political enemy, Louis T. Wigfall. Wigfall carried the cross for the South as far as he could. He served in the Confederate Army after Texas seceded. Then he was elected a member of the Confederate Senate. He fled to England when the South collapsed. He returned to Texas in 1872 and he died in Galveston in 1874. Sam Houston steered his own course. He knew which way the wind was blowing, but he continued to stand where he had always stood. He did not think slavery was an issue worth sacrificing the Union over.

Galveston had two labor unions by this time. The typographers and the carpenters were organized. They were the first labor unions in the state.

General E.B. Nichols came to Galveston in 1860 and bought John Sydnor's wharf for $20,000. Nichols had come to Texas from New York in 1837. He went into business in Houston with William Marsh Rice. They imported ice from New England, among other things. Rice did not approve of the purchase of the Sydnor wharf; so they split and Nichols stayed in Galveston. Nichols would say after the war that he was always a Unionist, but the secessionists mistook him for one of them.

The Democratic State Convention in Galveston wrote a platform in 1860 asserting the state's right to secede. Galveston voted overwhelmingly for the secessionist candidate, John Breckenridge, in the presidential election. Lincoln got no votes in Galveston. Moderates began leaning toward secession. Militants began buying guns and organizing military companies. Willard Richardson was denouncing Lincoln in the *News*. Stuart was suggesting in the *Civilian* that the South should wait and see how the Republicans behaved when they actually took office.

Galveston secessionists called a meeting to elect delegates to the secession convention they hoped would soon be convened. They chose Judge R.C. Campbell, John Muller and General E.B. Nichols. All three were believed to be uncompromising secessionists. Some people complained that harsh threats were used to prevent Unionists and moderates from attending the meeting where the delegates were chosen. The citizens of Galveston and Texas were split three ways. Some favored seceding and joining the other Southern states in a confederacy. Some favored seceding and becoming a republic again. Some favored staying with the Union. Feelings ran so high that people hesitated to discuss politics with their friends. The secession partisans were the most vocal. They intimidated the others. Few people spoke up against secession. Attorney William Pitt Ballinger did. He had helped engineer Lorenzo Sherwood's removal from the legislature over the slavery issue, but he did not think slavery was more important than the Union. Friends told Ballinger his stand against secession would embarrass his descendants.

He said he would take that chance. Ballinger said he was afraid Texas was doing an unwise and fatal thing.

Bishop John Odin moved to New Orleans to become bishop there in 1861 and C.M. Dubuis succeeded him as bishop of Galveston. Ferdinand Flake printed an article in his *Die Union* on January 5 deploring South Carolina's decision to secede. A mob broke into the *Die Union* office the same night and destroyed Flake's equipment.

Secessionist leaders in Austin issued a call on January 8 for a state convention to consider secession. Governor Houston tried to get out in front of the issue by calling the legislature into session. He made a speech against secession, but the legislature endorsed the call for a state convention. It convened January 28. Campbell, Muller and Nichols were there for Galveston. The convention voted for secession February 1 and scheduled a popular referendum for February 23. Texas voted for secession about three to one. The vote in Galveston was 765 for secession and 33 against it.

Many people thought the North would simply let the Southern states go. The British consul at Galveston thought that would happen and told his government so. Others expected war. Some were anxious for it and some were not. Sam Houston expected war and he dreaded it. Houston was removed from the governor's office by the Secession Convention. The convention never seriously considered returning Texas to the status of a republic. Sentiment was overwhelmingly in favor of joining the Southern confederacy. The convention notified the holders of state offices they would be required to swear an oath of allegiance to the Confederacy. Sam Houston declined to do it. The convention removed him and put Lieutenant Governor Ed Clark in the governor's office. Houston made no great outcry about it, but he decided he ought to explain his stand. He chose the state's principal city as the place to do it.

Houston arrived in Galveston April 19 by steamboat from Houston. A delegation of leading citizens met him at the dock and told him it would be better if he left. They said the public feeling against him was strong. Houston said he could not let the word go out that he had been intimidated. He went to the Tremont Hotel and started speaking from the second floor balcony. Accounts written at the time say the crowd was unfriendly but attentive. Houston reminded the crowd of what he had done for Texas.

This is part of the account Thomas North wrote about what Houston said about the outcome of the war he predicted:

> You may, after sacrifice of countless millions of treasure and hundreds of thousands of precious lives, as a bare possibility, win Southern independence, if God be not against you. But I doubt it. I tell you that, while I believe with you in the doctrines of state rights, the North is determined to preserve this union. They are not fiery, impulsive people, as you are, for they live in cooler climes, but when they begin to move in a given direction, where great interests are involved, such as the present issues before the country, they move with the steady momentum and perseverance of a mighty avalanche.

Houston told his listeners the time would come when their sons and husbands and brothers would be herded together like sheep or cattle at the point of a bayonet. He wished Texans were not doing what they were doing, but he said his sympathies would go with Texas whatever course it pursued. He probably did not change anybody's mind, but there was some scattered applause as he left. Houston was sixty-eight years old. He was still an imposing figure. His voice was still powerful. He had been out of step with his contemporaries before but never as far out of step as he was in 1861.

The Secession Convention established a committee to take charge of the U.S. property in Texas. Galveston's E.B. Nichols was appointed to the committee and made responsible for warships and any other federal property on the coast. General Nichols offered the crews of the U.S. ships equal rank in the Confederate forces. Some of them changed sides. *Civilian* editor Hamilton Stuart was the U.S.

collector of customs at Galveston. Nichols took over that office and the post office building that had just been completed. The euphoria lasted for several weeks. It began to wane when the first Union warship arrived off Boliver Roads to begin the blockade. The warship was the U.S.S. *South Carolina.*

It was plain to most people that Union forces could land at Galveston almost at will. Many people left the island and moved to Houston and other towns on the mainland. Willard Richardson moved the *Galveston News* to the mainland. Some other businesses moved, too. One writer estimated that forty percent of the population left.

The Union forces contented themselves with stopping ships until October, 1862. A Union force landed then and claimed the city. The Union troops never really occupied the town. They moved around some in the daytime, but they usually retired at night to fortified positions on Kuhn's Wharf. General Paul Hebert was removed from command of the Confederate forces in Texas because he let Galveston

The First National Bank of Galveston was organized immediately after the Civil War. The building the bank built in 1878 at the corner of The Strand and 22nd Street now houses an art gallery. The First National merged with Hutchings-Sealy in 1958.

go without a fight. His successor was General John Bankhead Magruder.

General Magruder was a Virginian and a graduate of West Point. He distinguished himself in the early fighting in Virginia and then made some mistakes during the Seven Days' Battle in June, 1862. His transfer to Texas was not a promotion. But he saw it as an opportunity to regain his reputation. He picked Galveston as the place to do it. He decided to take the city back with a night assault by land and water.

Magruder commandeered a little fleet of steamboats. He put troops on them and had them stack bales of cotton around the decks to serve as breastworks and also to make the boats look innocuous. He commandeered the rolling stock of the Galveston, Houston and Henderson Railroad and loaded the cars with all the men and guns he could round up. The general started his boats and troops moving toward the island after dark on New Year's Eve, 1862. Some history books say the Southerners recaptured the city in short order, capturing the Northern warship *Harriet Lane* and sinking the Northern warship *Westfield.* Other accounts say the battle lasted several hours. There were many mistakes and miscalculations on both sides and the Northerners sank the *Westfield* themselves. The Northerners evidently made the most mistakes beginning with their failure to watch the railroad. There is a detailed account in Charles W. Hayes' *History of the Island and the City of Galveston,* published in 1879. Hayes was working as a journalist and he had been in Galveston several years when he wrote his book. But some allowance perhaps should be made for his background. He was born in Pennsylvania. He was in the Union Army and he spent part of the war in a P.O.W. camp in Alabama. He said he got a lot of his information from Judge Peter Gray. The judge was a volunteer aide to General Magruder.

This version of the Battle of Galveston is taken from Hayes and from the *Galveston Tri-Weekly News* edition of January 3, 1863:

Magruder moved his troops and guns into the city under cover of night. He set up several artillery positions and gave the signal for the attack to begin by personally firing a cannon at 20th Street and The Strand in the direction of the Yankee ship *Owasco* in the harbor. The other guns started firing at the Yankee ships and at Kuhn's Wharf, where the Yankee soldiers were. The Confederate steamboats were out of position when the signal came and they were late joining in the attack. The Union ships had more firepower than the Confederates; so they had silenced most of the Confederate guns in the city before the Confederate steamboats got into the fight. The Confederate steamboats *Neptune* and *Bayou City* crashed into the Union gunboat *Harriet Lane*. The *Harriet Lane* ran the *Neptune* down and sank her. But the soldiers on the *Bayou City* swarmed onto the *Harriet Lane* and captured her. The captain of the *Harriet Lane* and most of the other officers were killed. The *Harriet Lane* had been a revenue cutter in the U.S. customs fleet before the war. Her first visit to Galveston had been to chase slavers. The skipper of the *Harriet Lane* killed in this battle was Jonathan Wainwright. His grandson years later would have to surrender Corrigedor to the Japanese in World War II.

Captain Henry S. Lubbock of the Confederate steamer *Bayou City* thought he could use the *Harriet Lane's* guns to force the surrender of the other Union ships. He took a skiff and a white flag and cruised over to the Union gunboat *Clifton*. Lubbock offered to accept the surrender of the Union fleet. Captain Law of the *Clifton* wanted to know what the terms were. Lubbock said the Yankees could keep one ship to carry their crews away and leave the rest with him. Law said he would have to clear it with Commodore William Renshaw. He was the senior Union naval officer in the harbor, but his flagship *Westfield* was unfortunately aground at the channel entrance. Renshaw would not surrender. He had three hours to reply to Lubbock's demand. The commodore decided to blow up his stranded flagship and sail the rest of the fleet out of the harbor. Renshaw and his crew set explosives on the *Westfield,* lighted the fuses and left the ship. It did not blow up when they expected it to. Renshaw and a few men rowed back to light the fuses again. The ship blew up and they were killed.

The rest of the Union fleet left the harbor. Some Confederates thought this was not sporting because there was supposed to be a truce in effect until the surrender deadline arrived. But the Confederates had compelled the Union troops on Kuhn's Wharf to surrender during all the excitement in the harbor; so the niceties were not being observed by either side that day.The Galveston, Houston and Henderson Railroad carried about 500 Union soldiers to a makeshift prison in a Houston warehouse and General Magruder was acclaimed a hero. He reported the loss of only twenty Confederate soldiers in the engagement. One of the Confederate casualties was Lieutenant Sidney Sherman. He was the only son of the San Jacinto veteran, General Sidney Sherman. Mourning with General Sherman was Confederate Major A.M. Lea. His son was killed in the fighting on the *Harriet Lane.* Lieutenant Commander Edward Lea was the executive officer on the Union gunboat. The Confederates repaired the *Harriet Lane* and used her as a blockade runner until the Union Navy recaptured her off Havana.

The Union came close to suffering a further loss at Galveston because communications were so poor. Another Union ship arrived off the harbor entrance on January 2. The steam transport *Cambriea* was carrying reinforcements for the Union garrison. General E.J. Davis was in command. He had not heard that the Confederates had taken the town back.

The Confederates tried to decoy the *Cambriea* into the harbor. They ran up the Union flag on two or three ships and buildings. The *Cambriea* sent a party of sailors into the harbor in a small boat to arrange for a pilot. The Confederates seized the Union sailors and sent a pilot boat out to lead the transport in. General Davis got suspicious. He took pilot John W. Payne prisoner and sailed back to New Orleans.

Confederates in Galveston identified one of the captured Union sailors as a deserter from the Confederate forces. They court-martialed him and shot him. General Davis did not know about this until much later. Some of his soldiers wanted to execute John Payne for trying to trick them.

Above: *The oldest surviving hospital in Texas is St. Mary's. It was established in 1866 as St. Mary's Infirmary. This building was built in 1875. It survived two great hurricanes, but the last section of it was demolished in the 1970s. A new St. Mary's occupies the site.*

Right: *Morris Lasker was one of the merchants attracted to Galveston by the commercial boom following the Civil War. He made a fortune from the Texas Star Flour Mills and real estate.*

Davis refused to allow it.

General Davis might have had very serious problems himself if he had entered Galveston harbor and been captured that day. He was born in Florida and he was a fairly prominent lawyer and judge in Texas before the war. Texans considered him the worst kind of renegade even before he became their carpetbag governor in 1869.

The Confederate raider *Alabama* sank the Union warship *Hatteras* off Galveston on January 11. The Union never tried to take the city again, but the threat was present throughout the remainder of the war. New fortifications were built and manned. But nobody believed the city could hold off a serious Union assault. The blockade was resumed January 7. Some ships managed to slip through to carry out cotton and carry back munitions and supplies. Many others were captured. The Union occupied every important Southern port except Galveston and Charleston and squeezed the life out of the Confederacy. Sam Houston probably never wanted to see his melancholy prediction come true and he did not. The Confederacy was wounded but still alive when Houston died in Huntsville July 26, 1863.

Confederate soldiers discovered some old coins in the sand while they were building breastworks on the beach during the last year of the war. The account in the *Tri-Weekly Telegraph* described the coins as Spanish doubloons. The paper said there were several thousand of them. Everybody supposed they were part of Laffite's loot. C.H. Leonard was mayor of Galveston when the war ended.

Confederate General Kirby Smith surrendered Texas to General E.J. Davis on June 2, 1865. The U.S. flag was raised over the city on June 5. The first elements of the occupation force began arriving June 16. General Gordon Grainger arrived to head the occupation forces on June 18. He issued the formal notice of the Emancipation Proclamation on June 19 and Texas slaves were freed. The provost marshal issued a notice urging freed slaves to make contracts with their former owners. The notice warned that the government was not going to support anyone able to work.

Ferdinand Flake suspended publication of *Die Union* during the war, but he published a newsletter he called *Flake's Bulletin*. Flake's influence increased with the occupation. He published the first official notice of the surrender terms. The *Galveston News* lost its press in a fire in Houston during the war. Willard Richardson bought the *Civilian* press from Hamilton Stuart and continued publishing the *News* in Houston until the war ended. He was still in Houston when Confederate veteran A.H. Belo came to him looking for a job. Richardson hired Belo as his business manager and took

Marcus McLemore built this big home in 1870 on 16th Street between Broadway and Avenue K. It became the Lasker Home for Children after the 1900 hurricane. That storm destroyed the orphanage that had been maintained by the Society for Friendless Children. The city and county helped the society buy this house. Morris Lasker donated the money to fix it up and furnish it. McLemore had died in 1898.

him back to Galveston. The *Galveston News* criticized everything connected with the occupation and the paper prospered. Hamilton Stuart acquired a new press and returned to Galveston to resume publication of the *Civilian* on July 5.

Citizens were returning to the city, too. Business houses were reopening and new businesses were moving in. The Union blockade was lifted in June. President Andrew Johnson re-opened the Southern ports to normal trade on July 1, 1865.

Many Texans still had cotton to sell. The demand was good and the money the cotton brought in was soon going out for equipment and consumer goods. Flake's *Bulletin* reported that the harbor was crowded with ships by the end of August. New businesses were opening in every available building and soon new buildings were going up. The federal courts were re-established. The federal government started building a new lighthouse on Bolivar Point. A.J. Alexander was appointed provisional governor. General Kirby Smith and General John B. Magruder went to Mexico rather than live under Union rule.

Units of the occupation force had offices in the Hendley Building, the Osterman Building and the Kuhn Building on The Strand and in the post office building. Some of the Union troops were quartered in the Tremont Hotel. The hotel caught fire the night of June 20. The balcony where Sam Houston made his speech and the rest of the building went up in flames.

Several Galvestonians prospered during the war by going somewhere else. Gail Borden's condensed milk made him rich. He stayed in the North and sold it to the Union Army.The Blum brothers moved to Matamoros and got rich from funneling Texas cotton through Mexico to the world markets. The Ball, Hutchings Company ran cargoes through the blockade. Robert Mills was a big blockade runner. He had business interests before the war in Havana and Europe. He ran his enterprise from outside the country during the war. Mills returned to Galveston after the war, but his business was soon in trouble. Much of his personal fortune had been tied up in slaves and in plantations that were of little use without slaves. Mills owed debts he could not pay. He went into bankruptcy. He sacrificed his home and personal property the law would have allowed him to keep. Mills won a lot of respect for his efforts to pay off his creditors, but he was ruined.

The Mills Company and Ball, Hutchings had been the big, unofficial banking houses in Galveston before the war. The city got its first national bank after the war. The First National of Galveston was the first national bank in Texas. It was organized in January, 1866, with T.H. McMahan as president.

The Galveston City Street Railway was organized the same year to operate horse cars. The first president was B.R. Plumley. Captain Haviland was mayor again. The U.S. Congress had not yet adopted the vindictive reconstruction measures. Southerners were reclaiming their civil rights and eligibility to hold office just by swearing an oath of allegiance to the United States. There was more crime than

Galvestonians were used to and there were some incidents between white citizens and black soldiers. But business was great. Traffic in the port during the first year after the war was twice as good as it had been in the best year before the war. The boom was attracting more entrepreneurs.

Morris Lasker moved to Galveston from Weatherford. He had come to Texas from Prussia in 1856. He worked for somebody else in Weatherford. He opened his own store in Galveston and made a fortune in dry goods and flour. Colonel William Lewis Moody moved to Galveston from Fairfield. Moody was born in Virginia. He had a law degree when he first came to Texas in 1856. Moody landed in Galveston and bought a horse to take him to Dallas, where he planned to open a law practice. The horse died on the way and left Moody stranded in Fairfield. He opened a law practice there and then went into merchandising. He became a successful cotton factor during the postwar boom in Galveston.

St. Mary's Hospital was established in 1866 and Galveston got its first medical school. The medical department of Soule University moved from Chappell Hill. The school changed its name to Galveston Medical College in 1871 and to Texas Medical College and Hospital in 1873. The school and hospital both closed in 1890 when the University of Texas Medical Department was established.

The Morgan Steamship Line resumed service to Galveston in 1866. The Texas and New York Steamship Company started a new service between Galveston and New York. This line was better known as Mallory or Clyde Mallory, after it absorbed the McMahon Line and the Williams and Guin Line.

General Gordon Grainger had been transferred to other duties and General Charles Griffin was the officer in charge of the Galveston occupation forces. Griffin removed Captain Haviland from the mayor's office and installed Isaac Williams in his place in June, 1867. General Griffin and his only son died a little later in the year of yellow fever. The epidemic that year was the last one in Galveston. Eight thousand people had the fever. Nearly 1,200 died. A hurricane that October killed three people and destroyed several buildings. Two thousand new homes were built that year. The first gas street lights were installed and Congress authorized some improvements to the harbor. P.J. and R.S. Willis moved to Galveston. The Willis brothers had come to Texas in 1836. They made their first money by cutting down trees and selling the wood to steamboat operators for their boilers. They opened a store in Montgomery and they were already prosperous before they came to Galveston and got rich.

The building boom continued in 1868. Work started on the Edward T. Austin home at 1502 Market Street. General Joseph Reynolds had succeeded General Griffin as head of the occupation forces in Galveston. General Reynolds removed General Griffin's man, Isaac Williams, and installed James McGee in the mayor's office. He also installed a whole new board of aldermen. Reynolds was the last occupation commander. He turned authority over to civilian officials in 1870 after he helped engineer the election of Republican E.J. Davis to the governor's office. Reconstruction was entering the hateful stage. Galveston was still relying on volunteer firefighters and they were not able to do much when fire broke out in December, 1869, in a big frame building on The Strand called Moro Castle. The fire destroyed that building and 100 others before it was put out.

A Galveston druggist named J.J. Schott was experimenting with chicle in 1869. Some accounts credit him with developing the first chewing gum. He never did anything commercial with it and he may not have been the first. Other accounts say the founder of the Adams Gum Company had started experimenting a few years earlier with some chicle he acquired from General Santa Anna while Santa Anna was in New York trying to get support for an effort to unseat the emperor Maximillian. That would have been during the Civil War. Work started in 1869 on a system of jetties at the entrance to Galveston channel.

The 1870 census gave Galveston a population of 13,818. It was still the biggest city in the state and the leading producer of manufactured goods. The depth of the channel at

Harris Kempner moved to Galveston in 1870. He went into the wholesale grocery business first, and then into cotton, banking and real estate. He was one of the founders of the Gulf, Colorado and Santa Fe Railroad. His descendants are still active in Galveston business and civic affairs. The Kempners developed the Imperial Sugar Refinery at Sugar Land.

Thomas Jefferson League built this commercial building in 1871 on part of the site that had been occupied by a big frame building known as Moro Castle. The earlier building had been destroyed by fire in 1869. This is the corner of The Strand and Tremont (23rd Street). It was in the heart of the commercial district in the 1870s. This building and most of the others in the area were neglected and run down until the restoration movement got started in the early 1970s. George Mitchell restored this building in 1979. Cynthia Mitchell's Wentletrap Restaurant occupies the ground floor.

105

the inner bar was ten feet. Harris Kempner moved from Coldspring to found one of the island's commercial dynasties. He had come to Texas from Poland in 1856.

The hero of the Battle of Galveston died in 1871. John B. Magruder came back to Texas after Maximillian was executed. He did some lecturing about his experiences in Mexico. He settled in Houston in 1869. He died there and he was buried there, but his remains were later moved to Galveston. Many important new buildings were going up. Thomas Jefferson League built a three-story brick retail and office building that still stands on The Strand at Tremont Street. The public school system was established. People were afraid the carpetbaggers were going to make whites and Negroes go to school together, but they did not. The first weather office in Texas opened in Galveston in 1871.There were just fifteen other weather offices in the country at the time. They were manned by the Army Signal Service. The Galveston Historical Society was organized August 3. It was reorganized as the Texas Historical Society in 1894 and then reorganized again as the Galveston Historical Society in 1942.

One of Galveston's citizens started a climb to political power in 1871 when the carpetbaggers made him sergeant-at-arms of the Texas legislature. Norris Wright Cuney was still in his twenties. He was born in Waller County. He was just fifteen when he came to Galveston in 1859, but he had been to school a while in Pennsylvania. Cuney started reading law in a lawyer's office in Galveston and he was one of the few educated Negroes around when the Republicans and carpetbaggers took over the state's affairs. He became a power in the Republican Party. He controlled the party in Texas in the 1880s and '90s, until 1896.

The legislature gave the governor power to appoint and remove local officials in 1872. This was to make sure no unreconstructed rebels held any office. Governor E.J. Davis removed General Reynolds' man, James McGee, from the mayor's office and installed Albert Somerville and another new slate of aldermen to run Galveston.

The Galveston building boom came under professional

Top: *The old Tremont Hotel was destroyed by fire while Union occupation troops were living in it in 1865. Galveston investors organized a company to build a new Tremont. They engaged a Memphis architectural firm to do the plans. The Memphis firm sent a young architect named Nicholas J. Clayton to supervise the work on the hotel and on the First Presbyterian Church building. Clayton decided to stay in Galveston. He was the first professional architect here and he designed many of the city's most distinguished buildings.*

Center: *The Tremont had a feature the Hyatt chain favors today. The lobby was open all the way to the top of the building and there was a skylight above it. This building was demolished in 1928.*

Bottom: *The steel lighthouse tower the Coast Guard built at Point Bolivar in 1872 still stands. But it has been dark for a long time. The Coast Guard turned the light out in 1933. The tower and the keeper's cottages are now privately owned.*

influence in 1872. The Memphis architectural firm of Jones and Baldwin was commissioned to design a new Tremont Hotel and a new building for the First Presbyterian Church. Jones and Baldwin sent Nicholas Joseph Clayton to Galveston to supervise the work. Clayton was born in Ireland. He grew up in Ohio. He served in the Union Navy during the Civil War, then joined the Memphis firm to study sculpture, engineering and architecture. He was just thirty-two when he arrived in Texas.

Galveston was as rich as any city its size anywhere. It was plain there would be plenty of work for architects in Galveston. There was no other professional architect present. Nicholas Clayton decided to spend the rest of his life in Galveston. The decision would bring more benefits to Galveston than to Clayton.

Galveston News editor Willard Richardson opened the Tremont Opera House in 1872. The Mallory Line started regular passenger steamship service between Galveston and New York. The Coast Guard replaced the Bolivar Lighthouse with the steel tower that still stands on Bolivar Point.

The major cotton factors started talking in 1872 about forming a cotton exchange. The Galveston Cotton Exchange was organized in 1873 with Colonel William H. Sellers as the first president. Galveston was full of colonels. Sellers had earned his rank with Hood's Brigade.

Galveston already had had its last serious bout with yellow fever, but no one knew that at the time. People still worried about yellow fever and the worry sometimes produced quarantines. The cotton and much of the other cargo coming to the port of Galveston was coming by rail by this time. The only railroad came through Houston. Houston boosters were doing everything they could to get shippers to use their port. Galvestonians noticed that the yellow fever quarantines Houston sometimes slapped on traffic between the two cities diverted profitable business from the port of Galveston to the port of Houston. They suspected the quarantines had more to do with commerce than they had to do with health.

Galvestonians decided they needed a railroad that did

not go through Houston. They chartered the Gulf, Colorado and Santa Fe Railroad in 1873 to provide direct access between the cotton country and the Galveston waterfront. The founders were the Sealy brothers, W.L. Moody, Moritz Kopperl, Henry Rosenberg, Albert Somerville, C.R. Hughes, Harris Kempner, Walter Gresham, Leon Blum, Julius Runge, R.S. Willis, H.A. Landes and John C. Wallis. The line was planned to run west of Houston up through central Texas and the Panhandle to connect with the Denver and Rio Grande at Santa Fe. Work started in May, 1875. The railroad created new towns. Some of them were named for people connected with the railroad. Rosenberg and Moody were named for stockholders. Temple was named for the railroad's chief engineer, Bernard Temple. The Gulf, Colorado and Santa Fe built a branch line from Alvin into Houston in 1882. The company was absorbed into the Atchison, Topeka and Santa Fe in 1886.

The Galveston, Houston and Henderson line had connections with other railroads by 1873 that allowed passengers to travel by train to faraway places like Kansas City and New York. John P. Davie built the Washington Hotel at 2228 Mechanic Street.

Galvestonians got to vote in a city election in 1873 for the first time in six years. They elected C.W. Hurley to the mayor's office. F.W. Schmidt opened a beer garden at Avenue O and 20th Street that became one of the city's most popular recreation spots. The Wharf Company built the first grain elevator.

Hamilton Stuart sold his *Civilian* in 1874 and went to work for Willard Richardson at the *Galveston News*.Their differences always were more political than personal. The *Galveston News* was still the most important paper in the state with a big circulation outside the city.The city got a second trolley system in 1874. The Peoples' Street Railway was organized to run horse trolleys into areas not being served by the Galveston Street Railway Company. Leon Blum was one of the organizers of the Peoples' line. The Army Corps of Engineers started work that year on improving the jetty system at the harbor entrance.

The issue of a seawall was raised for the first time in 1875. A major hurricane brushed past Galveston and wrecked the city of Indianola on September 16. Indianola was a busy port on Matagorda Bay. It had no protection. Nearly 300 people were killed. Hundreds of homes and buildings were destroyed. The *Galveston News* pointed out that Galveston had no more protection than Indianola had. The paper advocated building a seawall. The city council voted $5,000 for storm protection, but that was not enough for

The city's large German population established a social club in the 1870s at 27th Street and Avenue O. They called it the Garten Verein. It has been known as Kempner Park since Stanley Kempner bought it and donated it to the city in 1923. The dancing pavilion designed by Nicholas Clayton had to be rebuilt after it was damaged by fire in 1979.

a seawall. Galveston interests did prevail upon the delegates to the 1875 Constitutional Convention to write into the new state constitution a provision for tax rebates to help communities finance projects like seawalls. Nothing was done about building a seawall, but the Army Signal Service adopted the red and black hurricane warning flag that year.

The Mallory Line was the dominant concern in the shipping business by 1875 with direct service to the East Coast, England and Germany. The second railroad trestle to the mainland was completed by the new Gulf, Colorado and Santa Fe line. R.L. Fulton was mayor.

Willard Richardson died in 1875. Richardson had made A.H. Belo a partner earlier. Belo and a couple of associates took over control of the *Galveston News*. They reorganized the company the following year and that was the beginning of the A.H. Belo Company.

The city's German families established the Garten Verein social center on the property that is now Kempner Park. Nicholas Clayton finished work on the First Presbyterian Church and designed a new central tower for St. Mary's Cathedral. The city charter was amended to give each of the twelve aldermen his own district.

A new railroad passenger depot was completed in 1876 by the Galveston, Houston and Henderson line. It was on Water Street between 23rd and 24th streets. Galveston got rail service to San Antonio in 1877. The line that had started as Buffalo Bayou, Brazos and Colorado became the Galveston, Houston and San Antonio. The Galveston, Houston and Henderson connected with it at Harrisburg.

The Galveston, Houston and Henderson passenger station was at 24th and Water Street on the waterfront from 1876 until 1889. It was a busy place. Passengers and freight could get on and off the island then only by rail or boat.

Top: *The Galveston Cotton Exchange built this building in 1878. This picture evidently was made a few years later because it shows the* Galveston News *building next door, left. The* Galveston News *building was not finished until 1884. This is the corner of 21st Street and Mechanic. The exchange demolished this building in 1941 and built a new building about the same size. The* Galveston News *building still stands, but it has been plastered over and it is unrecognizable.*

Center: *Members of the Cotton Exchange posed for this picture when their original building was new. This handsome room was sometimes used for balls and social events.*

Bottom: *The Galveston City Railway started operating street cars drawn by mules in 1866. A second company called the Peoples' Street Railway started operating in 1874. The Galveston City line absorbed the Peoples' line in 1879.*

Opposite: *One of Nicholas Clayton's most spectacular Galveston buildings was Harmony Hall. It was built for a Jewish social club at Church and 22nd Street in 1881. It was later occupied by a business school and then by a Scottish Rite lodge. Howard Barnstone said this building would have attracted attention even in Paris in the 1880s. It was destroyed by fire in 1928.*

The First National Bank started the building that still stands at the corner of 22nd Street and The Strand. D.C. Stone was mayor.

The new Gulf, Colorado and Santa Fe Railroad reached Arcola in 1878. A.H. Belo installed the first telephone line in Texas. It connected Belo's home at 1 Avenue K with his office at 113 Market Street. The channel entrance had been deepened to twenty feet at the inner bar. Several more major brick buildings were completed, including the Produce Building on The Strand and the Cotton Exchange at 21st Street and Mechanic.

The first telephone exchange in Texas began operating in Galveston in 1879. C.H. Leonard was mayor. The Peoples' Street Railway Company merged with the Galveston City Street Railway Company. The resulting company kept the Galveston City name. The company had fifty employees, thirty cars and 140 mules. The office and stable were at the corner of 21st Street and Avenue I. The fare was five cents.

The strongest labor organization in Galveston was the

Above: *An elite corps of longshoremen worked on the cotton docks in Galveston during the last twenty or thirty years of the nineteenth century. The cotton compresses of that day were not very efficient. The bales of cotton were not really tightly packed when they reached the docks. The members of the Screwmen's Benevolent Association specialized in squeezing and jamming the bales into the holds of the cotton ships.*

Opposite: *Real estate dealer Henry Trueheart had Nicholas Clayton design this building for him in 1882. The Galveston Junior League restored it in 1971. It is on 22nd Street just off The Strand behind the First National Bank Building.*

Screwmen's Benevolent Association. The members were specialists in jamming cotton into ships. A crew of screwmen could get ten or fifteen percent more cotton into a ship than an unskilled crew could. The screwmen were all white. They would not work for any concern employing Negroes. Black longshoremen formed a Cotton Jammers' Association in 1879, but whites monopolized the waterfront jobs until 1883. The Screwmen's Association eventually affiliated with the Longshoremen's Union. There was not much call for their services after 1910 because the cotton compresses were much more efficient by then.

The census of 1880 put the population of Galveston at 22,248. It was still the biggest city in Texas. Trade was increasing about as fast as the population. The volume of wholesale and retail trade combined was $30 million in 1880. This was an increase from $18 million in 1870. The big Galveston business houses were the biggest business houses in Texas. Some of the big wholesalers were the Blums and the Willises in dry goods and the Browns in hardware. The

Galveston Tribune started publishing in 1880.

Signs of changes to come were already appearing. The development of cotton compresses and railroads gave cotton shippers other choices. More factories were being built inland, where raw materials were handier. Houston would displace Galveston as the chief manufacturing center in Texas by the end of the eighties. The Wharf Company was creating big problems for the future by charging rates most people thought were unreasonable and by expanding the port at a rate that would later be judged too slow. The third railroad trestle was completed to the mainland by the Galveston, La Porte and Houston Railway in 1880. One of the big social events of the year was a reception at the Tremont Hotel for Ulysses S. Grant. The ex-president was making a grand tour of the country and Galvestonians made sure he saw all the local sights, including the view from the lookout tower on top of the Tremont. The reception and dinner for Grant was supposedly the occasion where Grant's Civil War lieutenant, Philip Sheridan, made his famous

remark about which place he would live in and which place he would rent out if he owned Hell and Texas. Sheridan was no stranger to Texas. He had served on the border before the Civil War and he managed the occupation of Louisiana and Texas for a while right after the war.

The Galveston City Railway Company built the first bathhouse on the beach in 1881. It was an elaborate frame building designed by Nicholas Clayton. The company called it the Electric Pavilion. Electricity was new. One of the big attractions at the Electric Pavilion was an electric light. People paid to see it. They paid to use the bathhouse and they paid to ride the trolley there and back. The Electric Pavilion was a big success. It stood on the site where the Moody Convention Center is now until it burned in 1883. The Galveston public school system got on a firmer footing in 1881 when voters approved a school tax. L.C. Fisher was mayor.

The Brush Electric Company began offering electric service to homes and businesses in Galveston in 1882. A number

of lawyers held a meeting at the Electric Pavilion in July and organized the Texas Bar Association. Judge Thomas J. Devine was elected president. The association met in Galveston every year for the first several years of its existence. It folded after the legislature created the State Bar of Texas in 1939.

Some of the new business buildings completed in Galveston in 1882 were the Trueheart Building on 22nd Street off The Strand, the W.L. Moody Building at 2202 Strand

Opposite: *The street car company was looking for ways to get more riders on the trolleys in the 1880s. The company built a big bathhouse and entertainment center on the beach. This was called the Galveston Pavilion in the beginning. It was called the Electric Pavilion after the first electric light went on display here. The building was made entirely of wood and it made a big blaze when it burned in 1883.*

Right: *W.L. Moody, Jr. started the American National Insurance Company in an office in this building W.L. Moody, Sr. built in 1882 on The Strand at 22nd Street. The Moodys did their cotton and banking business here, too, in the early days. They no longer own the building. It is occupied by a merchant dealing in surplus military equipment and clothing. The building originally had a fourth floor. It blew off in the 1900 storm.*

Bottom: *Nicholas Clayton designed this building for the Galveston Artillery. The Artillery started as a volunteer military organization and evolved into a private club. It is located now at Avenue O and 30th Street. This building was at Sealy and 22nd Street.*

and the Kaufman and Runge Building at 230 22nd Street.

Galveston civic leaders organized a Deepwater Committee to promote the port.

Twenty Dominican sisters arrived in Galveston in 1882 to start the Sacred Heart Convent at 16th Street and Market. The sisters also operated the Cathedral School. They moved their mother house to Houston in 1927. The Missouri-Pacific and the Missouri-Kansas and Texas railroads acquired the Galveston, Houston and Henderson line in 1882.

The beach Galveston's great Beach Hotel stood on is now underwater. This was the finest resort on the Texas coast when it was new in 1883. The building burned two years before the 1900 hurricane sucked this part of the beach out to sea.

The original company no longer owns or operates any rolling stock in its own name. It is still a corporate entity, though, and its charter is the oldest in Texas. It was issued in 1853. The Buffalo Bayou, Brazos and Colorado was chartered three years earlier, but that company has been absorbed into the Southern Pacific system.

Galveston had a few electric street lights in time for the 1883 Mardi Gras celebration. Nicholas Clayton designed a hall for the Galveston Artillery at 22nd Street and Sealy.

A longshoremen's strike in 1883 gave Norris Cuney the opportunity to put black longshoremen on the docks. He made sure they were paid the same rates as white longshoremen.

The first big resort hotel opened on the Galveston beach in 1883. The Beach Hotel was a gaudy four-story frame affair with wrap-around verandas and a dome. The site, on the beach at Tremont Street, is beyond the seawall now and under water. Nicholas Clayton designed it and it was the fanciest resort in Texas.

The *Galveston News* moved into a new brick building on Mechanic Street in 1884. This is said to have been the first building in the country designed specifically to house a newspaper plant.

Ball High School was completed the same year at 21st Street and Ball. The street and the school were named for George Ball. He donated $50,000 to pay for the school. John Sealy died and left $50,000 for a hospital.

W.L. Moody, Walter Gresham, Julius Runge and H.A. Landes started a new railroad in 1884. The Galveston and

Ball High School was named for George Ball because he donated $50,000 to help pay for the original building. George Ball came to Galveston in 1839 and went into the dry goods business with his brother, Albert. He made most of his money after he established a banking house with John Sealy and John Hutchings in 1854.

Top: *Ball High School was the most elegant public school in Texas when it was new in 1884. It stood at Ball and 21st Street. The site was crowded with additions before the school was moved to the present larger site. The original building was demolished to make way for the insurance company office that occupies this site now.*

Bottom: *This house somehow survived the big fire of 1885 that burned most of the buildings in a forty-block area in the east end. This was the home of Wilbur Cherry. He was one of the founders of the* Galveston News. *The house was built in 1852 at Church and 16th Street.*

Western line was intended to run down the island, across San Luis Pass and through Corpus Christi to the Valley. It never got off the island. The Galveston and Western line was completed from the waterfront out the island to Laffite's Grove, where the Pirates' Beach subdivision and the Galveston Country Club are today. The western end of this line was abandoned after the 1900 hurricane washed the tracks away. The company shut down and sold its remaining assets to the Santa Fe in 1923.

The English sailing bark *Elissa* docked in Galveston for the first time in 1884. She hauled a cargo of cotton to Liverpool.

The city established a paid fire department in 1885. The department's first real test came that November when a fire started in the Vulcan Iron Works at 16th and The Strand. It spread to surrounding buildings and, before it was put out, it destroyed most of the buildings in the forty blocks between the port and the beach. Four hundred families lost their homes.

The Sweeney-Royston house on the corner of Avenue L and 24th Street is a private museum owned by the Paul Powells. James M. Brown had this house built in 1885 for his daughter Mathilda when she married Tom Sweeney. The marriage did not last. Mathilda moved back to the Brown home on Broadway. Sweeney continued to live here for a while and Mathilda did not sell the place until after Sweeney died. It was the home of Judge Mart Royston after that.

One of the most ornate frame houses ever built in Galveston was started right after the 1885 fire destroyed so many of the island's frame buildings. This house at Sealy and 19th Street was originally the home of the Jacob Sonnentheils. The Stubbs family lived here for a long time after the Sonnentheils. Former mayor Ted Stubbs grew up in this house. It was restored in 1977 by the Lee Trenthams.

The fire had little effect upon Galvestonians' bias toward frame homes. Nicholas Clayton finished work in 1885 on a frame house at 24th Street and Avenue L for J.M. Brown's daughter.

The A.H. Belo Company established a branch in Dallas in 1885. Belo sent an employee named George Bannerman Dealey to publish the *Dallas Morning News.* That paper has been published by the A. H. Belo Company ever since, but no one named Belo has had anything to do with it since George Dealey and associates bought out A.H. Belo's heirs in 1926.

The new owners of the *Civilian* could not compete with the *Galveston News,* so they closed down Hamilton Stuart's old paper in 1886. W.L. Moody, Jr. turned twenty-one and became a partner in the W.L. Moody Company. Work started in 1886 on the most extravagant home ever built in Galveston. The Walter Greshams moved a frame home from the corner lot at 14th Street and Broadway and commissioned Nicholas Clayton to build them a castle on the

Top: *Pictures of the aftermath of the 1900 storm show this house standing like a rock amid the wreckage of other buildings. It has withstood every hurricane since the 1900 storm and it has been referred to as the Bishop's Palace since 1923 when the Catholic Church bought it as a residence for the late Bishop Christopher Byrne. The house is now headquarters for the Newman Club of Galveston and it is open to visitors for a fee.*

Bottom: *The mansion H.A. Landes built on Postoffice at 16th Street had intricate wrought- iron trim around the porches. The iron was being replaced when this picture was made in 1983. Landes was a merchant and cotton man. He was mayor from 1905 til 1909.*

Top: *A picture of this house is on the cover of Howard Barnstone's book about Galveston's architecture. This was the residence of John Darragh. He moved here in 1886, but Barnstone thinks it was not a new house. He says the architect apparently combined two older houses and added a cupola and some towers and the gallery. The fence is about the most imposing feature of the Darragh house. Darragh was president of the Wharf Company when he lived here at 519 15th Street.*

Below left: *The house George and Magnolia Sealy built at 25th Street and Broadway is one of the four or five finest houses in Galveston. It was occupied by Sealys until Robert Sealy died in 1979. It passed, then, to the University of Texas Medical Branch. The school will use it as a conference center. George Sealy was John Sealy's younger brother. Magnolia Sealy was the daughter of merchant P. J. Willis. John Sealy, Jr. gave her name to the oil company he organized in 1911. Magnolia Petroleum was later absorbed into Mobil.*

site. Clayton was said to have felt the site was too small for the house the Greshams wanted. He built it, anyway, and it has been one of Galveston's principal ornaments ever since it was finished in 1893.

The Landes house at 1604 Postoffice Street was built in 1886 for wholesale grocer H.A. Landes.

A second hurricane struck Indianola in 1886. It wiped the town out. It was never rebuilt. The *Galveston News* said it was another warning for Galveston, but some people had

Opposite right: *Henry Cohen was rabbi of Temple B'nai Israel from 1888 until he retired in 1949. He was a special friend of immigrants and an advocate of prison reform. He took a leading part in the relief work after the 1900 storm and in nearly every other civic endeavor in Galveston. Rabbi Cohen was 89 when he died in 1952.*

Above: *Another rich Galvestonian gave the school system a school in 1888. The Rosenberg School was paid for by banker Henry Rosenberg. The school was at 11th Street and Winnie. It was demolished in 1965. There is a new Rosenberg School on the site now.*

Top: *This building on Mechanic was built in 1888 to house the Leon and H. Blum dry goods business. George Mitchell owns the building now. He is converting it into a hotel. He will call it the Tremont House.*

Center: *The new city hall built in 1889 was elaborate on the east end where the city offices were and plain on the west end where the police and fire departments were. This building was badly damaged by the 1900 storm and some of the trim never was replaced. The fire and police departments remained here after the present city hall was built in 1916 until this building was demolished in 1962. The ground floor was originally a farmers market.*

Bottom: *The old Tremont Hotel dominated the commercial district when the city celebrated its fiftieth birthday in 1889. This was Market Street in its heyday.*

Morris Lasker's real estate business and flour mill had made him rich by the time he built this mansion at 1728 Broadway. Morris and Nettie Lasker's son, Albert, grew up in this house. He was a reporter for the Galveston News *and the* Dallas Morning News *before he went to Chicago to join the Lord and Thomas Advertising Agency.*

Albert Lasker eventually gained control of Lord and Thomas. John Gunther called him the father of modern advertising. He helped develop the radio soap opera and orchestrated the promotion of Lucky Strike cigarettes. The Lasker house was demolished in the 1960s.

persuaded themselves that Galveston was not in the path of the killer hurricanes. A Navy oceanographer had once advanced such a theory. People wanted to believe it. Nothing was done about a seawall.

Work started in 1887 on another great showplace on Broadway. Nicholas Clayton was the coordinating architect on the site. But the George Sealys wanted something really out of the ordinary, so they got New York architect Sanford White to draw up the plans for the mansion they called Open Gates. It was occupied by Sealys continuously until 1979.

Henry Cohen came from England in 1888 to become rabbi of Temple B'nai Israel. Cohen served the temple for sixty-four years. He also supported every civic endeavor and became the most popular man in Galveston. President Woodrow Wilson once called him the First Citizen of Texas. Henry Rosenberg built the Rosenberg School for the Galveston school system in 1888. Leon and H. Blum put up a new three-story building in the 2300 block of Mechanic

Street to house their thriving wholesale dry goods business.

There was a big celebration in 1889 marking the fiftieth anniversary of the founding of the city. There were parades and speeches, carnival attractions and military maneuvers. The little Galveston and Western Railroad ran excursion trains from downtown to the festival site, approximately where the Army would later build Fort Crockett.

The city government put up a new city hall in 1889 and it stood for sixty-five years right in the middle of 20th Street

Right: *Nicholas Clayton designed this home in 1890 for J.C. League. It was later the home of the Kempner family for many years. The house still stands at 1702 Broadway.*

Below: *The Galveston City Railway started buying electric trolley cars in 1889. But the conversion was delayed by the 1900 storm and the last mules were not retired until 1905.*

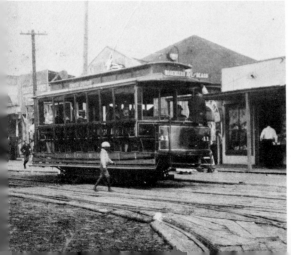

between Market and Mechanic. Nicholas Clayton proposed a design, but the city chose another one submitted by Alfred Muller. Clayton never approved of it.

President Benjamin Harrison came to visit the island in 1889 and Governor James Hogg came down from Austin to welcome him. Shippers and merchants in the middle part of the country were agitating for a new deepwater port west of New Orleans. They held meetings in 1883, 1888 and 1889 trying to agree on a plan they could present to Congress. Most sentiment favored Galveston. Congress decided in 1889 to let the War Department decide which site was best.The War Department started a study in March and reported in December that Galveston was the best site. Congress voted money to improve the jetties and authorized further improvements to the harbor the following year. The channel entrance was deepened to twenty-six and a half feet over the next seven years. Electrification of the trolley lines began in 1889.

Galveston probably had its finest hours in the 1890s. The census of 1890 showed that Dallas and San Antonio both had passed Galveston in population. Galveston had 29,084 people. Galveston still was the principal port and trading center and the city never was more prosperous. A second opera house opened in 1894. Renowned performers like Oscar Wilde, Edwin Booth, Sarah Bernhardt, Otis Skinner, John Phillip Sousa and Lily Langtry appeared at the Grand Opera House throughout the nineties. W.L. Moody, Jr. married Libbie Rice Shearn of Houston. She inherited substantial real estate in Houston. Moody urged her to sell it because he was sure Houston would never amount to anything.

Classes started in 1891 at the new University of Texas Medical Department. The voters of Texas had chosen Galveston as the location for the first state medical school after the legislature authorized it in 1881. Nicholas Clayton designed the original school building and the original John Sealy Hospital building. The Medical Department had thirteen teachers and twenty-three students that first year. It operated as the University of Texas Medical Department until 1919 when the name was changed to University of

Top: *John Sealy's executors decided to use the money he left to build a teaching hospital for the University of Texas Medical Department the legislature had authorized in 1881. Nicholas Clayton designed the building and the John Sealy Hospital was finished by the time the medical school started conducting classes in 1891.*

Bottom: *Nicholas Clayton also designed the original classroom building for the University of Texas Medical Department. This is the Ashbel Smith building, also known as "Old Red." The original hospital building was replaced a long time ago, but the Ashbel Smith building is being restored.*

One of the most impressive buildings ever built on the island was the Ursuline Convent, designed by Nicholas Clayton in 1891. The 1900 storm damaged the buildings and destroyed the brick fences. The Convent and the Ursuline Academy were damaged again by Hurricane Carla in 1961. The sisters decided the buildings were too far gone to be repaired. They were demolished in 1962.

Texas Medical Branch. It is now the biggest employer on the island by far. But commerce was still in the ascendency in the 1890s. Commerce was making Galvestonians rich and rich Galvestonians were pouring money into new homes, churches, schools and business buildings. Nicholas Clayton had all the work he and several helpers could handle.

Clayton designed a new building for the Clarke and Courts office supply house in the 2100 block of Mechanic and a new building for Marx and Blum in the 2300 block of The Strand in 1890. He designed the Central High School building and the Ursuline Academy and a new federal courthouse in 1891.

Clayton produced the plans for St. Mary's Cathedral School and the Sacred Heart Church in 1892. He designed the Grace Episcopal Church in 1894.

Clayton's firm produced the plans in 1895 for the John Sealy and the Ball, Hutchings buildings on The Strand and for a new wharf and warehouse for the Mallory Line. Probably no architect ever had as much influence on the

The first high school for Negroes in the state was established in Galveston in 1885. Nicholas Clayton designed this building to house the school in 1891. This was Central High School. The building still stands at 27th and Avenue M, but it was enlarged and remodeled almost beyond recognition in 1924. The school district built a new Central High at Sealy and 30th Street in 1954. It ceased to be a high school in 1968 when all the Galveston schools were integrated. Ball High is the only public high school on the island now. This building now houses a Community Action office and a branch library.

appearance of a city as Nicholas Clayton had on the appearance of Galveston.

The *Handbook of Texas* says the Daughters of the Republic of Texas organization was established in Houston in 1891. Galveston historians hold that the idea was conceived by William Pitt Ballinger's daughter, Betty, in the library of the Ballinger home. The library was saved and moved to the corner of 29th Street and Avenue O½ to be preserved when the Ballinger home was demolished.

Galveston has had three federal buildings. Two of them still stand. This one does not. It was built in 1891. It was demolished in 1935 when the present federal building was built on the same site on 25th Street between Winnie and Church.

Top: *Nicholas Clayton designed the Grace Episcopal Church in 1894 and the building was completed in 1895 at Avenue L and 36th Street. This is one of the Galveston buildings listed in the* National Register of Historic Places.

Bottom: *This little building at 29th Street and Avenue O½ was once part of the home of attorney William Pitt Ballinger. It was Ballinger's library. It was saved and it is maintained by the Daughters of the Republic of Texas because the idea of the DRT was born here.*

People traveling between Galveston and the mainland before 1893 had to take the train or a boat. The first wagon bridge was completed that year between the island and Virginia Point on the mainland.

Henry Rosenberg died in 1893 and left most of his large fortune to be used for the benefit of Galveston. His greatest gift was the Rosenberg Library. Rosenberg's money also paid for the Texas Heroes' Monument at Broadway and 25th Street, for several fountains around the city and for the

Top: *They called this the longest wooden bridge in the world when it was built in 1893. The iron framework rested on concrete piers, but the roadway was made of wood. There were only railroad trestles before. This was the first bridge to the mainland.*

Right: *Banker Henry Rosenberg left no children when he died in 1893, but he left evidence of his devotion to Galveston everywhere. He left part of his fortune to be used for a public library. The Rosenberg Library stands at 23rd and Sealy with Rosenberg's likeness outside the main entrance.*

Letitia Rosenberg Home for Women. Letitia Rosenberg was Henry Rosenberg's first wife. He married again after she died in 1888, but he had no children. Dr. A.W. Fly was mayor in 1893.

Two communities developed on the west end of the island in the 1890s on the Galveston and Western rail line. South Galveston was a resort community on Lake Como about where the Galveston Country Club is. It had about 3,000 people at one time. Nottingham was about a mile east of

Lake Como. There was a lace factory at Nottingham. The South Galveston and Gulf Shore railroad was chartered in 1891 to build a rail line to the west end of the island, but it was abandoned in 1896. It would have been wiped out by the 1900 storm as the Galveston and Western line and the settlements of South Galveston and Nottingham were.

C.J. and N.C. Jones chartered a new railroad in 1894, to connect Bolivar Point with Beaumont. They called the railroad the Gulf and Interstate and part of their plan was

Right: *Rosenberg's will also provided money for a monument to the heroes of the Texas Revolution. The monument was placed here at the intersection of 25th Street and Broadway in April, 1900. Young adventurers from Houston used to joke that the statue on top was pointing the way to the red-light district. Actually the hand is pointing more nearly toward the Rosenberg Library.*

Below: *Rosenberg money paid for the Letitia Rosenberg Home for Women on 25th Street. The home opened in 1895 and closed in 1976. The building is now privately owned. It was damaged by Hurricane Alicia in 1983.*

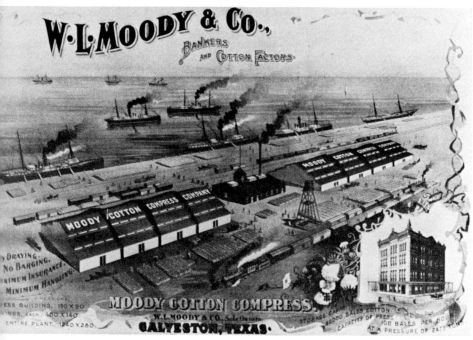

Top: *There was a little town once about where Constable Sam Popovich is standing. The town was called Nottingham. It was on what is now Stewart Road near Eleven Mile Road. A few remnants of the foundation of the lace factory that was the town's main industry are visible in the pasture here.*

Bottom: *The first cotton compress on the Galveston waterfront was built in 1894 by Colonel W.L. Moody.*

Opposite: *The first jetties at the Galveston harbor entrance were made of pilings. A system of stone jetties was completed in 1896. The engineers built rail lines into the Gulf and hauled granite out on flatcars.*

136

to develop a port at Bolivar. The railroad company changed hands a couple of times and went through receivership once before it folded in 1934, but the rail line was built down the Bolivar Peninsula before 1900. Trains were ferried across the harbor entrance on a barge in the early 1900s. The trains stopped at Bolivar Point before that and transferred their passengers and freight onto a ferry boat.

W.L. Moody built the first waterside cotton compress in Galveston in 1894.

There was a rare snowstorm in Galveston in 1896. The snow was fifteen inches deep in some places. The possibility of another kind of storm continued to worry a few people. An engineer named Joseph Eads was brought in to advise the city how to protect itself from the sea. Eads recommended building a dyke and filling in the lower places in the city. Galvestonians already had been filling in low places. They often took sand from the dunes for fill. So the island did not even have the little natural protection the dunes would have afforded. No dyke was built. Most Galvestonians

continued to depend upon Providence for their protection.

New stone jetties authorized by Congress were completed at the channel entrance in 1896. The city by this time was pumping most of its water from wells at Alta Loma on the mainland. The water in the wells on the island had turned salty.

The Galveston County Courthouse burned in December, 1896. Nicholas Clayton submitted plans for a new courthouse and they were accepted. Clayton got the contract. He posted a bond of $80,000 and left town to tend to some other business. There has been a dispute ever since about what happened next and about who was to blame. The county built the new courthouse, but county officials complained about the plans and seized Clayton's bond. The county and the architect were fighting for years. Clayton never recovered his money. The loss and the fees he had to pay former governor James Hogg and his other lawyers kept him poor until he died. The publicity reduced the demand for his services, but Clayton continued to work the rest of his life. One of his most spectacular creations was destroyed one night in the spring of 1898. The Beach Hotel burned to the ground. One eyewitness said the flames were so hot, the firemen could not get close enough to put water on them. The firemen then had steam pumpers pulled by horses. The steam pumps boosted the water from the fire hoses farther than it would have gone without them, but it was not far enough that night. The hotel would have lasted only another two years, anyway. It never could have withstood the 1900 hurricane.

The new Galveston Brewery and Ice Company plant started making High Grade brand beer in 1897. The brewery switched to ginger ale and root beer during Prohibition and came out with Southern Select Beer after Repeal.

The Army bought the land between 45th and 53rd streets from the beach back to Avenue U in 1897 and started building Fort Crockett. It was named for the Alamo hero, David Crockett. It was designed for coastal defense, but it was used first as a staging area during the Spanish American

Opposite: *The courthouse Galveston County built in 1899 was a public shelter during the storms of 1900, 1915 and 1961. The building was damaged by Hurricane Carla in 1961 and demolished in 1965 to make way for the present courthouse. This photograph of the 1899 building was made about 1939. This was the county's fourth courthouse. The first one was built in 1838* on *The Strand at 17th Street. The second was built in 1848 on this site and the third one was built in 1856, also on this site.*

Above: *The Galveston Brewery and Ice Company opened in 1897 at 33rd and Church Street. The company's advertising described its High Grade brew as "the beer that is a food."*

Top: *Galveston had the first
country club in the state. The
original golf course, established
in 1898 on 45th Street near the
beach was wiped out by the 1900
storm. The club rebuilt on 52nd
Street and moved in 1919 to a
site on 61st Street at the beach.
The club sold the 61st Street site
to the city after World War II
and moved to the present site
on Stewart Road at Lake Como.*

Bottom: *Galveston was the
busiest and most prosperous city
in Texas by the end of the
nineteenth century.*

Opposite: *Galveston was
handling more cotton than any
other port in the United States
in 1900. The city was no longer
the largest in Texas, but the
economic future never looked
brighter.*

War and the border troubles with Mexico.

The Galveston Country Club was organized in 1898.

Galveston was the number one cotton port in the nation at the end of the 1890s. Only four ports were handling more tonnage. Galveston was at the peak of its prosperity and influence. Many Galveston families had become very wealthy. The wealthiest were the Moodys, the Sealys, the Kempners, the Hutchings, the Willises and the Balls. The mayor at the turn of the century was Walter Jones.

The census of 1900 put three cities ahead of Galveston in population. The Galveston population was 37,788. Dallas, San Antonio and Houston had more people. Houstonians were aggressively going after shipping business, but Galveston still was the only deepwater port. The Galveston port was handling 1,200 ships a year. The city had twenty hotels and sixty factories.

PART FOUR

Disaster and Recovery 1900-1957

The Mayans had a god for every purpose. The god of thunder and lightning and evil winds was called Huracan in the Quiche dialect. We have changed the spelling, but we have not found a better word for evil winds. Hurricanes had no names or numbers in 1900. The U.S. Weather Service was still in its infancy. It had been moved from the Army Signal Service to the Department of Agriculture in 1891. The Weather Service office for Galveston was in the Levy Building. The man in charge was Dr. Isaac Cline. The hurricane that would be the greatest tragedy Cline and Galveston ever endured passed over Santo Domingo and Port au Prince on September 1, 1900. The storm crossed Cuba and headed for Key West.

The Weather Service issued its first bulletin on September 4 while the storm was still in Cuba. All points along the Gulf Coast between Biloxi and Brownsville were alerted on September 6. Isaac Cline raised the ominous black and red warning flag in Galveston on September 7. The first mention of the storm appeared in the *Galveston News* the same day. It was Friday. The sun was shining on Galveston. Rain started falling on Saturday morning and the wind was soon rising. A few people left the island. Most people followed their normal routine. There was no emergency plan. Some people took the trolley out to the beach to watch the waves. There were three large bathhouses on stilts on the beach. The waves were soon tearing away pieces of these buildings, but the sightseeing excursions continued until the rising tide undermined the trolley tracks. The afternoon train from Houston got in two hours late because of the high water.

The 1900 storm punished the city for fifteen hours, from the afternoon of September 8 until the morning of September 9. This is all that was left of the Jesuits' Sacred Heart Church at Broadway and 14th Street on the highest part of the island.

145

Passengers on the afternoon train from Beaumont had a longer delay. The Gulf and Interstate train made it to Bolivar Point, but the wind and the tide were so strong the ferryboat *Charlotte Allen* was unable to dock. The *Charlotte Allen* turned back to Galveston. The train started backing toward Beaumont. Some of the passengers hopped off and took refuge in the Bolivar Lighthouse. Many residents of Bolivar sought shelter in the tower too. More than 100 people sat out the storm there.

The average elevation in Galveston in 1900 was four and a half feet. The highest ground in the city was at Broadway and 15th Street. It was eight and a half feet above sea level. Many houses near the beach were only two feet above sea level. Some of the residents of those houses left and took shelter in sturdier buildings on higher ground, but many chose to stay with their houses. The owners of sturdy houses, including the elegant mansions, took in as many refugees as they could accommodate.

The telegraph lines between the island and the mainland

went down shortly after 4:30 Saturday afternoon. The last message was a weather bulletin reporting half the city under water with the wind blowing fifty miles an hour. The velocity was seventy-four miles an hour at 5 p.m. It was eighty-four miles an hour fifteen minutes later just before the anemometer blew away. No one knows how hard the wind blew at the height of the storm. It may have been 150 miles an hour. The water rose twelve feet or more. Furious waves broke up buildings large and small. Some buildings strong

Opposite: *The federal weather office for Galveston was on the third floor of the Levy Building at Market and 23rd Street in 1900. It was here that weatherman I. M. Cline issued the hurricane warning on September 7. This photograph evidently was made a few years later. There were no cars on Galveston streets in 1900. The Levy Building is known now as The National Hotel Building. It was built in 1871, remodeled for the Levy Company in 1895 and remodeled again in 1954 for the National Hotel chain. The Levy/National Hotel Building was originally the Tremont Opera House. The remodelers lowered the first floor ceiling by about seven feet and concealed all the original cast iron support columns. The columns are still visible in the machinery space* above the present first floor. A developer has been talking about buying this building and restoring the first floor.

Above: *The storm derailed freight cars and wrecked warehouses and tore ships from their moorings. The wharf area was a shambles on the afternoon of September 9. The wagon bridge and the three rail trestles to the mainland all were wrecked. But the port was back in limited operation by the 17th. One railroad trestle was rebuilt and trains were running in and out of Galveston again by the 21st.*

enough to withstand the wind and the waves were battered down by the debris from wrecked buildings. Roof tiles and sheets of tin roofing sailed through the air like shrapnel. Some people saved themselves by clinging to floating wreckage. Many could not save themselves. Isaac Cline lost his wife and two children when their house at 25th Street and Avenue Q collapsed. The roof of the Grand Opera House caved in. The top floor of the Moody Building blew away. Ten nuns and ninety children were killed when St. Mary's Orphanage was wrecked. The new Sacred Heart Church in the highest part of town collapsed. The third floor of the city hall was wrecked and the first floor was flooded, but most of the refugees in the building survived by huddling on the second floor. The skylight fell in at the Tremont Hotel. Saint Mary's Hospital lost all its windows, but the building survived. Hundreds of people rode out the storm there. One of the many heroes of the storm was a young intern named Zachary Scott. He rescued several elderly women from an old folks home and carried them to safety at St. Mary's. Scott later became a specialist in tuberculosis. He started the sale of Easter Seals in Texas. He was the father of the movie actor, Zachary Scott.

The storm lasted for fifteen hours. The water receded quickly after the wind died down. Whole blocks of houses had been reduced to kindling. Many of the surviving buildings had gaping holes in their walls and many were roofless. It would later be estimated that 3,600 homes were destroyed. No exact count of the dead ever could be made because disposition of the remains became an emergency

Opposite: *It is not easy to exaggerate reports of a disaster that killed 6,000 people, but some of the journalists of the day managed to do it. Some accounts in the national press spoke of dozens of looters being shot. Galveston accounts put the number at six or seven.*

Bottom: *The First Baptist Church was demolished by the storm. This was the second building the Baptists had built on this site. They built another one after the storm and then demolished it after they built the present church on the adjoining site, facing 23rd Street, in 1958. This corner is now a parking lot.*

Top: *St. Mary's Catholic Orphan Asylum was right on the beach at 57th Street. The storm wiped out every building near the beach and moved the beach back as much as two blocks in places. The frame buildings of the orphanage were splintered. Bodies of nuns and children were found afterward all over the area. Many of the bodies were tied to each other with ropes. The nuns apparently tried to save the children by tying groups of them together. Each nun tied herself to a group of children.*

and many bodies were burned. Probably 6,000 people died.

Help obviously had to be obtained. The railroad trestles and the bridge to the mainland had been destroyed. The telegraph lines were down. Richard Spillane of the *Galveston Tribune,* Lawrence Elder and four other men volunteered to carry the word of the disaster to the mainland. The Moody family's yacht, *Pherabe,* somehow had survived the storm. Spillane and his party went to Texas City on the yacht Sunday morning. They found a railroad hand car and rode that

Right: *Mayor Walter Jones took strong measures against looting and price gouging and got Galvestonians to work clearing the debris and disposing of the dead.*

Below: *State guardsmen commanded by Brigadier General Thomas Scurry put the city under martial law.*

150

Red Cross founder Clara Barton came to inspect the damage and stayed to supervise the relief work.

until they met a train and transferred to it. The party made it to Houston about midnight Sunday and sent telegrams from there to Governor Joseph Sayers and President William McKinley telling them that Galveston needed food, clothing and money at once. Help was soon on the way. Red Cross founder Clara Barton came to Galveston to direct her agency's efforts personally.

The concern and compassion the citizens showed for each other during the storm was less evident in the aftermath. Everything was scarce. Prices shot up. The fare for a boat trip to the mainland jumped from $1.50 before the storm to $8.00 afterward. Mayor W.C. Jones took some drastic measures. He organized a committee of public safety. He gave L.R.D. Fayling power to raise and command an emergency force to patrol the city and keep down looting. Fayling's men shot several suspected looters. The looting and shooting reports were badly exaggerated by some elements of the press. The mayor imposed price controls. He took charge of the food supply . He decreed that anyone

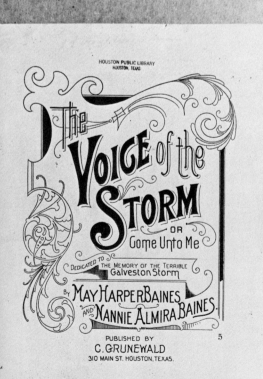

THE GREAT
GALVESTON DISASTER

CONTAINING A

Full and Thrilling Account of the Most Appalling Calamity of Modern Times

INCLUDING

VIVID DESCRIPTIONS OF THE HURRICANE AND TERRIBLE
RUSH OF WATERS; IMMENSE DESTRUCTION OF DWELL-
INGS, BUSINESS HOUSES, CHURCHES, AND LOSS
OF THOUSANDS OF HUMAN LIVES;

THRILLING TALES OF HEROIC DEEDS; PANIC-STRICKEN MUL-
TITUDES AND HEART-RENDING SCENES OF AGONY;
FRANTIC EFFORTS TO ESCAPE A HORRIBLE
FATE; SEPARATION OF LOVED ONES, ETC.

Narrow Escapes from the Jaws of Death

TERRIBLE SUFFERINGS OF THE SURVIVORS; VANDALS
PLUNDERING BODIES OF THE DEAD; WONDERFUL EX-
HIBITIONS OF POPULAR SYMPATHY; MILLIONS
OF DOLLARS SENT FOR THE RELIEF OF
THE STRICKEN SUFFERERS

BY PAUL LESTER
Author of " Life in the South-West, Etc., Etc.

With an Introduction by
RICHARD SPILLANE
Editor " Galveston Tribune" and Associated Press Correspondent

PROFUSELY EMBELLISHED WITH PHOTOGRAPHS
TAKEN IMMEDIATELY AFTER THE DISASTER

PHILADELPHIA, PA.:
CHARLES FOSTER PUBLISHING CO
716 Sansom Street

HOUSTON PUBLIC LIBRARY
HOUSTON, TEXAS

The
VOICE of the
STORM
OR
Come Unto Me

DEDICATED TO THE MEMORY OF THE TERRIBLE
Galveston Storm

BY MAY HARPER BAINES
AND NANNIE ALMIRA BAINES

PUBLISHED BY
C. GRUNEWALD
310 MAIN ST. HOUSTON, TEXAS.

5

Left: *The news of the Galveston calamity got enormous play in newspapers and magazines all over the world. Several publishers rushed into print with books about the great storm.*

Below: *There was even a song about the tragedy. The refrain was:"Oh, the Angel of death has pass'd o-ver . . . And stricken that beautiful City . . . and snatch'd many thousands of lov'd ones, . . . from Galveston's waterbound shore . . . and stricken that beautiful city . . . on Galveston's waterbound shore."*

Opposite: *The seawall the Galveston News had advocated twenty-five years earlier was an obvious necessity after 1900 if people were going to continue living on the island. The city and county called in engineers and got a bond issue approved and went to work. The original section of the seawall started at the harbor, followed 6th Street to the beach and then ran along the beach to 39th Street. The extension that protects the eastern tip of the island was not added until later.*

refusing to help clean up the wreckage and dispose of the dead would not eat.

General Thomas Scurry brought in 200 state volunteer guardsmen. They put the ruined town under martial law. They evacuated some of the homeless to Houston and set up tent cities for the others.

There is little mention of it in the history books, but two members of the Moody family recall that there was some talk about abandoning the island and starting a new Galveston on the mainland after the great storm. W. L. Moody was in New York when the storm struck. W.L. Moody, Jr. and his family were in Galveston. Mary Moody was just eight years old. She remembers the storm, but she seems to remember better how her father and grandfather felt about the idea of moving the town. She said they both said they would stay on the island regardless of what anybody else did. She said they both loved to hunt and fish and they thought the hunting and fishing would be better with fewer people. W.L. Moody III also recalls his father saying he hoped some of the others would move, but he would not.

The Southern Pacific had taken over Charles Morgan's railroads and the Morgan Steamship Line in the 1880s. Southern Pacific was building some expensive new docks in Galveston when the storm hit. The docks were damaged and all the rail lines were washed out. The railroad owners took the same attitude the Moodys did. Repairs began immediately.

The idea of moving the town never got beyond the

conversation stage, but the business leaders did decide some changes had to be made. The city government had been conspicuously inefficient for many years. It was always in debt and always issuing revenue bonds to cover expenses.

The Deepwater Committee petitioned the legislature to change the form of government. The committee was made up of business and civic leaders able to get the legislature's attention. The leaders were I.H. Kempner, R.W. Smith and Ed Cheeseborough. They proposed that Galveston be governed by four commissioners and a mayor-president. The legislature agreed. Three members of the commission were appointed by the governor in the original arrangement and two were elected. This was changed in 1903 to provide for election of all five commission members. The commission had a mandate to get Galveston back on its feet and the power to do it. Each of the four commissioners had control over a city department. There was a commissioner in charge of finance and revenue, another in charge of water and sewers, another was responsible for the streets and public property and one headed the fire and police departments.

Galveston is credited with inventing the commission form of government. It has its weaknesses. Galveston eventually abandoned it, but it was a good system for the time.

A party of business leaders took the train to New York in 1901 to persuade holders of the city's bonds to make some concessions on the interest so the city could reduce taxes for a time. George Sealy was a member of that delegation. He died on the train.

The new city government hired General H.M. Robert and

Opposite: *The contractors placed this granite marker on the seawall when they finished their work in 1904. It still stands at the seaward end of 23rd Street beside what is left of Murdock's Pier.*

Above: *The seawall was much more protection than Galveston had before, but the engineers said the elevation of the land behind the seawall should be raised, too. Dredgeboats were brought in from the low countries of Europe to pump sand from the bottom of the channel and the harbor and spread it over the city.*

two other engineers to devise some means of protecting the city from future storms. They recommended a seawall about three and a half miles long from the east end of the island to Fort Crockett. They estimated the wall would cost $1.5 million. They said the wall would not help much unless the elevation of the city was raised, too. The engineers estimated this would cost another $2 million. There was little controversy about it.

Galvestonians approved a bond issue to raise the money to begin work on the seawall. They got the state to agree to rebate taxes for thirty-five years to help them finance the grade raising and they started looking for contractors. The J.M. O'Rourke Company began work on the seawall on October 27, 1902, and finished the job July 30, 1904. The seawall was built of sand, cement and stone around a network of pilings and reinforcing bars. This original section was sixteen feet wide at the base and seventeen feet tall. Big blocks of granite from the same Hill Country quarry that furnished the stone for the state capitol were placed in front of the wall to break the force of the sea.

The Goedhart and Bates engineering firm started work on raising the elevation of the island about the same time the first section of the seawall was finished. The contractors dredged a canal into the heart of the city. They built dikes around sections of the city, then filled the sections with silt their dredges sucked up from the bottom of the bay and the Gulf. The filled areas took weeks and months to dry out. Residents had to walk to and from their houses on frame catwalks. The fill simply spread under the houses that had been built well above ground level. Many other houses, churches and business buildings had to be raised and the owners had to pay for that. Some sizable masonry buildings were jacked up to new elevations. It was a phenomenal effort. San Franciscans rebuilt their city after the earthquake. Galvestonians rebuilt their city and also made an island out of what had been only a sand bar. It probably was a mistake to build a city where Galveston was built. The people of Galveston corrected the mistake. They did it by themselves.

Below: *Galvestonians lived like the residents of some South Sea island fishing village while the saturated fill dried out. The grade-raising was not finished until 1910.*

Opposite: *The population of Galveston shrank. Thousands died in the storm and a few thousand others moved away rather than live with the possibility of another disaster. There was a buyers' market in real estate. W.L. Moody, Jr. was one of the people to benefit from it. He bought the R.S. Willis mansion on Broadway for a fraction of what it had cost to build. Some reports said he paid $20,000 for this place. He lived here until he died. His older daughter still lives here.*

No one knows what Bernardo de Galvez had in mind when he chose the motto "Yo solo" for his coat of arms. But it is difficult to think of a motto more appropriate for the city that took his name. "Yo solo" is Spanish. It translates to "I alone."

The grade raising took six years. It was finished in July, 1910. All the streets had to be rebuilt. Utilities had to be relocated. All the planting had to be done over. Life in Galveston was not easy, but businessmen did not neglect their businesses.

Some business houses opened on the Monday following the storm. Wreckage was cleared away from the docks. Ships were moving in and out of the harbor again in a few days. Work started on a new railroad trestle to the mainland.

Some people were so frightened by their experiences during the storm or so devastated by the loses they suffered that they left the island. There was more real estate for sale than there were buyers. W.L. Moody, Jr. was able to buy the R.S. Willis mansion on Broadway for a fraction of its value.

Galvestonians were preoccupied with their own problems when A.F. Lucas brought in his gusher at Spindletop. Houston cashed in on the oil boom and became the principal oil port and refinery center. Some people believe Galveston might have captured more of this business if Spindletop had happened at another time.

W.T. Austin was mayor of Galveston in 1901. The Rock Island Railroad began service to Galveston in 1902 using the same tracks as the Santa Fe. The only connection between the island and the mainland was one railroad trestle. Automobiles had to be carried to and from the island by train, but automobiles began to appear in Galveston. Dr. Seth Morris of the University of Texas Medical Department is said to have been the first islander to have his own car. It was an Oldsmobile. Simon and Tobias Sakowitz established in Galveston in 1902 the dry goods business they would later move to Houston. The Lykes Brothers Steamship Company opened an office in Galveston in 1903.

The Rosenberg Library opened in 1904. The city closed

Opposite top: *Thomas Lucas was one of the first apartment builders in Galveston. The block of brick flats he built near the beach before the storm was demolished by the 1900 hurricane. Lucas built this apartment house in 1901 in the 1400 block of Broadway on the higher ground, farther from the beach. Rose Trost sold this building in December, 1983, to Robert Lee Kempner Lynch. He plans a full restoration.*

Opposite bottom: *The building occupied for the past eighty years by the Galveston Children's Home has been bought by developer J.R. McConnell. He probably will turn it into apartments or offices. The Galveston Children's Home has merged with several other children's institutions. The original children's home on this same site was destroyed by the 1900 storm. Publisher William Randolph Hearst staged a bazaar in New York to raise the money to build this building in its place. It faces 21st Street between avenues M and M½.*

Above: *The Jesuits built a new Sacred Heart Church on the same site that had been occupied by the church the storm destroyed. The earlier building was designed by Nicholas Clayton in 1884 and completed in 1892. A Jesuit architect designed this building. It was started in 1903 and finished in 1904. The 1915 storm destroyed the dome and the present dome was designed by Clayton. It was one of his last projects.*

Left: *W.L. Moody, Jr. was forty years old when he and I.H. Kempner formed the American National Insurance Company in 1905. Moody had complete control of the company four years later. He ran it personally until he died in 1954.*

Maco Stewart formed the Stewart Title Company in 1907. Stewart was born in Galveston in 1871. His father was Judge William Stewart. The judge had moved to Texas from Maryland in 1844. He settled in Galveston in 1869. Maco was named for his two half-sisters, Mary and Cora Stewart.

the municipal library and moved all the books from it to the Rosenberg Library. The municipal library had been the first one in Texas. It was chartered in 1874.

W.L. Moody, Jr. and I.H. Kempner reorganized in 1905 a little insurance company they had bought the previous year. They renamed it American National Insurance Company and opened an office in the Moody Building on The Strand. The insurance company lost money for several years. Moody bought out Kempner's interest in 1909. The legislature about the same time passed a law requiring insurance companies doing business in Texas to invest seventy-five percent of their reserves in Texas. Some big national companies did not want to do that; so they left. It was a bonanza for Texas companies like American National. The hard feelings between Moodys and Kempners that colored Galveston's commercial and political life for many years may have started about this time. W.L. Moody, Jr. was born in Fairfield. He was one year old when his parents brought him to Galveston.

Above: *The Stewart Title Company bought the Kaufman and Runge Building at Mechanic and 22nd Street. Stewart Title has since become a large national concern. The company still owns this old building and keeps it in better than new condition. Kaufman and Runge were coffee importers and cotton merchants. They built this building in 1882.*

Left: *The first black man to win the heavyweight boxing title was Jack Johnson of Galveston. He was boxing here while prize fights were still illegal in Texas. Governor Joseph Sayers sent the Texas Rangers to Galveston once in 1901 to stop a fight between Johnson and Joe Choynski. The Rangers arrested both fighters and put them in jail.*

The Galveston City Railway Company completed the conversion to electricity in 1905 and the mules were retired. H.A. Landes was mayor. He was a merchant and cotton broker. He had served with the Confederate forces defending Galveston during the Civil War. Maco Stewart and his brother, Minor, bought the Kaufman and Runge Building in 1905 and made it headquarters for the first title company in Texas. The Stewarts both were lawyers. They had bought up a couple of small abstract companies. They started writing title insurance as a partnership in 1905 and they chartered the Stewart Title Company in 1907.

The volume of cotton exports was up to three and a half million bales by 1906. The federal government finished work that year on an extension of the seawall to protect Fort Crockett. W.L. Moody, Jr. organized the City National Bank in 1907. He was president. Soon afterwards he organized the American Bank and Trust Company and made his son president. W.L. Moody III was the youngest bank president

Right: *Americans were becoming obsessed with speed in the early 1900s. Somebody hatched an idea for a race between an airplane and an automobile on the Galveston beach. Charles K. Hamilton flew the plane. George Sealy, Jr. drove the Marmon automobile. They raced in 1912, but the caption that appeared with this picture failed to say who won.*

Below: *The only bridge between Galveston and the mainland after the 1900 storm was the railroad trestle rebuilt right after the hurricane. There was no bridge for wagons and cars until 1911.*

in the country at the time. He was nineteen years old. He said his father fired him for being too reckless in lending the Martini theaters the money to buy a pipe organ.

The city staged the first Cotton Carnival in July, 1908. There were auto races on the beach and beauty pageants to attract tourists to the island.

Maco Stewart bought into the Galveston City Company in 1909. Lewis Fisher was mayor.

Jack Johnson knocked out Jim Jeffries in Reno in 1910 to become the first Negro heavyweight boxing champion. Johnson was born in Galveston in 1878. He worked on the docks and started his boxing career at the Union Club on 22nd Street at Church.

The population of Galveston was increasing again. The census of 1910 put the total at 36,981. Galveston was the sixth largest city in the state. It was a popular tourist resort again. What happens on the freeway on Sunday mornings now was happening then on the railroads. All the lines serving Galveston ran excursions from Houston on Sunday

Opposite: *The county and railroads built a causeway in 1911. It was concrete, stronger than the previous bridge and trestles had been, but the 1915 hurricane damaged it and put it out of service for a time.*

Above: *The new causeway was such an improvement that people did not complain for a long time about having to stop every time the lift bridge had to be opened to let a tugboat pass.*

mornings. The trains raced to be first to cross the bay. There were three sets of tracks, but only one trestle. The railroads cut back on their excursion schedules when the Galveston-Houston interurban service started in 1911. The inaugural run of the interurban coincided with completion of a new causeway between the island and the mainland. It was all concrete. It had two lanes for cars and tracks for the trains and the interurban electric trains. Galveston had not been as closely linked to the mainland since the 1900 storm wiped out the 1893 wagon bridge. Galveston County built the causeway and paid one quarter of the cost. The railroads and interurban company paid the rest. The railroads are still using this causeway.

The federal government was building a new immigration and quarantine station on Pelican Island in 1911. Immigrants were landing in Galveston at the rate of 5,000 a year. The city had four incorporated banks and six private banks.

The Galvez Hotel opened in 1911 to provide visitors with

Above: *The 1911 causeway had a separate set of tracks for the new electric interurban trains that began running between Galveston and Houston that year. The downtown terminal was on 21st Street, but there was also a stop at Offatt's Bayou where the race track was.*

Opposite top: *The causeway and the interurban made it possible for more people to visit Galveston more easily. Galveston investors built the Galvez Hotel in 1911 to accommodate the visitors. This picture of the Galvez was made in 1983 after the hotel had an expensive overhaul and before Hurricane Alicia smashed some of the windows and blew off some of the roof tiles. The Galvez still looks much the same as it did when it was new.*

Opposite bottom: *Galvestonians in businesses connected with tourism did not wait for tourists to discover the island. There was vigorous promotion. The caption that appeared with this picture in a promotional brochure said the Galveston beach was the finest and safest bathing beach in the world.*

fancier accommodations than had been available on the beach before. The main backers of the hotel were the Galveston City Railway and I.H. Kempner.

More than four million bales of cotton moved through Galveston in 1912 and the port was second in the nation in tonnage. American National Insurance Company built a new building at 21st Street and Market. Twenty-six passenger trains were coming in and out of Galveston every day by 1914. The Galveston, Houston and Henderson was running a *Galveston News* Special every morning carrying newspapers for the subscribers on the mainland. Galvestonians were big travelers. They could reach New York by train in about forty hours. Some preferred the Mallory liners. They made it in about a week. Steamer time to Europe was about twenty-five days, but World War I soon ended that service. The Houston Turning Basin and Ship Channel were finished in 1914. The immediate impact on Galveston was barely noticeable, but it was the beginning of the end of the Galveston monopoly. Brownsville, Corpus Christi, Freeport,

Beaumont, Port Arthur, Orange and Texas City all were developing deepwater ports, too.

Another hurricane struck the island in August, 1915. It was a major storm. Wind gusts reached one hundred and twenty miles an hour. The water rose so high that a schooner was swept over the seawall onto Fort Crockett. Sections of the new causeway washed away and there was some property damage, but the seawall held. Most of the buildings withstood the storm. Only eleven people were killed.

Opposite: *Galveston suffered another setback in 1915. A hurricane probably as fierce as the 1900 storm swept over the city. Many buildings were damaged, but there was little loss of life. The seawall held, but the boulevard broke up and washed out. This picture apparently was made at about 11th or 12th Street. The building in the far background is the Galvez Hotel.*

Above: *W.L. Moody, Jr.'s elder daughter has been known as Mary Moody Northen since she married E.C. Northen in 1915. The Northens started their married life in a new brick home at 2902 Broadway. Mrs. Northen moved back to her father's house after Northen died in 1954. This house has been vacant ever since.*

King Vidor was captivated by pictures when he was growing up in Galveston in the early 1900s. He was making home movies when most people his age were just learning to work the Kodak. Young Vidor moved to Hollywood in 1915 and had a long career as a director. Vidor worked with many of the big stars. He directed Northwest Passage, Duel in the Sun, The Fountainhead, Ruby Gentry *and many other successful films. Vidor was born in Galveston. He died in California in 1982.*

Opposite center: *The city government left the fire and police departments in the old city hall building on 20th Street and moved to this building on 25th between Winnie and Sealy in 1916.*

Galvestonians had proof of the value of the investment they had made.

W.L. Moody, Jr.'s daughter Mary married insuranceman E.C. Northen in 1915 and became Mary Moody Northen. Northen came to Galveston from Cass County in 1904. He died in 1954.

King Vidor left Galveston in 1915 and moved to California. King was born in Galveston in 1894. He started making pictures with a Kodak when he was a youngster, and he was making moving pictures by the time he was in his teens. He also worked as a ticket taker and projectionist for one of the early Galveston movie houses. Vidor was just twenty-one when he and his bride and a comedian named Edward Sedgwick drove to California in his Model T. Mrs. Vidor was Florence Arto. She was soon getting parts in feature films. Vidor was directing feature films by 1918.

The great architect, Nicolas Clayton, died in 1916. He accidentally set fire to his clothing while he was trying to trace a crack in his chimney. He caught pneumonia while he was recovering from the burns and the pneumonia killed him.

The Moodys split their operations into the W.L. Moody Cotton Company and W.L. Moody, Bankers. The city built a new city hall and work started on the Crystal Palace bathhouse on the seawall in 1916.

I.H. Kempner was mayor when the United States entered the World War in 1917. It was not called World War I then because people believed there would not be another

Left: *The mayor of Galveston during World War I was Isaac H. Kempner. He was the eldest son of Harris Kempner. The Kempners were highly respected. I.H. Kempner was popular with many Galvestonians, but not with the Moodys. Kempners and Moodys regularly took opposite sides in city elections until the 1950s.*

171

one. This was the war to end wars. Isaac Kempner was the son of the Polish immigrant, Harris Kempner. He inherited his father's interests in cotton, banking, sugar and real estate. He was president of the Galveston Cotton Exchange for eighteen years.

The garrison at Fort Crockett grew to about 3,000 soldiers plus a couple of detachments of Marines during the war. News of the armistice reached Galveston early on the morning of November 11, 1918. People took an undeclared holiday. There was an impromptu parade. The war had not been good for business. Shipping traffic declined substantially. It increased rapidly after the war ended. The business of the port doubled between 1919 and 1920. The seawall was extended to the eastern tip of the island to protect more of the city and the Fort San Jacinto coast artillery base. Maco Stewart gave the federal government a large tract of land on the beach to get the government's cooperation on the extension.

Galveston never was a hotbed of temperance, but the

Opposite top: *Soldiers were trained at Fort Crockett during World War I to handle heavy artillery. The fort was built in 1897. It was inactive after 1900 until it reopened in 1911 as a mobilization center during the skirmishes on the Mexican border.*

Opposite bottom: *There was a small Army airfield in the early days of military aviation on 61st Street at Stewart about where the K-Mart store is now.*

Right: *The City National Bank built a new building on the same site it had been occupying in the 2200 block of Market Street. The City National was merged eventually into the Moody National Bank. Mary Moody Northen then gave this building to the Galveston County Museum.*

island had to go along when prohibition fever seized the country in 1918. The movement had been around for some time. There were state-wide elections on prohibition in 1887, 1908 and 1911. Texans voted against it all three times, but 199 counties had voted dry in local option elections before 1918 when the U.S. Congress voted to submit the Eighteenth Amendment for ratification. Ratification was not completed until January, 1919. But the Texas legislature voted for ratification February 28, 1918, and then immediately enacted a state law to stop the sale of alcohol in Texas.

Drinking never was outlawed during Prohibition. It was legal to have alcohol and legal to drink it. It was illegal to sell it and illegal to transport it. It was not illegal to buy it. Drinking continued in Galveston and everywhere else. Bootlegging never was really respectable, but patronizing bootleggers was perfectly acceptable and quite chic. Galvestonians were seldom without something to drink. The late Al Scharff said in the book he and Garland Roark wrote about his career that he was aware his in-laws were buying booze from somebody. He apparently did not try to find the source. Scharff was the customs agent in Galveston when bootlegging was big business. He had married Ida Nussbaum. Her brothers were prominent merchants.

The Galveston Dry Dock and Construction Company established a shipyard in 1919. Galveston merchant Robert I. Cohen bought out Foley Brothers Dry Goods Company of Houston in 1919. Cohen came to Galveston from England in 1877. He worked for Levy and Weis until he opened his own store in 1889.

W.L. Moody, Jr.'s City National Bank put up in 1919 the building that still stands at 2219 Market Street. Dr. H.O. Sappington was mayor.

Horse racing lost some of its appeal when the legislature outlawed betting on the results in 1909. But the Galveston Downs horse track was still operating near Offatt's Bayou in 1920. The track was converted to a dog track before it finally closed down.

The Texas legislature passed a law against betting on horse races in 1909. Most race tracks closed. Galvestonians, characteristically, continued to go to the races and bet on the horses. Galveston Downs was still operating on Offatt's Bayou in the 1920s. It was converted to a dog track and then closed before betting became legal again in 1933.

Above: *One of the famous aces of World War I came to Galveston in 1921 as a member of the Dusenberg race team. Eddie Rickenbacker, center, and his colleagues were competing in the Cotton Carnival races.*

Below: *The auto races on the beach were just part of the hoopla of the annual Cotton Carnival. The Cotton Carnival was just part of the ballyhoo program Galveston promoters generated to draw more tourists to the island.*

Galveston was still the sixth biggest city in Texas. The population was 44,255, according to the census of 1920. W.L. Moody died in 1920. Clark Thompson started the Cedar Lawn subdivision on a site near 45th Street and Avenue K that had once been a swamp. Clark Thompson was married to W.L. Moody, Jr.'s younger daughter, Libbie. The Thompsons had a home in Cedar Lawn. Mrs. Thompson's brother, Shearn Moody, did too. Mainlanders like to settle near the water when they come to Galveston. Galvestonians seem

BOULEVARD AND BATH HOUSES
GALVESTON, TEXAS

Top: *The promotion paid off. The seawall and the bathhouses were jammed on summer weekends all through the 1920s.*

Center: *Surfing and sunbathing hadn't caught on. The big thing was just to get in the water. Many visitors plainly were satisfied just to get close to the water, with all their clothes on.*

Bottom: *These were the prize winners in the 1927 bathing beauty contest. These beauty pageants were promoted vigorously. At one time the Galveston contest was called the International Pageant of Pulchritude.*

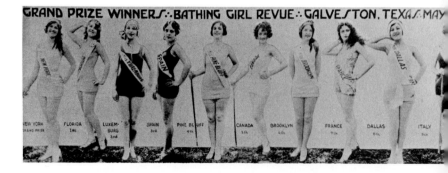

GRAND PRIZE WINNERS ∴ BATHING GIRL REVUE ∴ GALVESTON, TEXAS, MAY

NEW YORK GRAND PRIZE   FLORIDA 1st   LUXEM-BURG 2nd   SPAIN 3rd   PINE BLUFF 4th   CANADA 5th   BROOKLYN 6th   FRANCE 7th   DALLAS 8th   ITALY 9th

to favor locations out of sight of the water. Nothing about Cedar Lawn in any way suggests that there is a beach nearby.

C.A. Keenan was mayor in 1920. A young Italian named San Jacinto Gaido opened a seafood restaurant on Murdock's Pier on the seawall. San Jacinto came to Galveston with his parents when he was two. He became one of the big boosters of the Galveston beachfront. The present operators of Gaido's Motel and Restaurant on the seawall are his descendants.

Galveston was exporting more grain than any other American port by 1921. The volume that year was seventy-five million bushels. The port was second only to New York in total tonnage in 1923. Repairs to the causeway were completed in 1922 and people could drive to Galveston again.

W.L. Moody, Jr. took over all the Moody empire after his father died. He merged his American Bank and Trust Company into W.L. Moody Company and moved the company into his American National Building. W.L. Moody III held several offices in the Moody companies at this time, but he and his father fell out again a few years later.

Bootlegging and rumrunning were well established by the early twenties. Al Scharff said the operators were divided into two camps by 1924. There was a beach gang run by Sam and Rose Maceo and a downtown gang run by George Musey.

Al Scharff said Musey brought some of his liquor in by truck from Louisiana. The Maceos brought most of theirs in by boat. Both organizations employed the services of

One of the people least impressed by the beauty pageants was Catholic Bishop Christopher E. Byrne. He denounced them as immoral. The bishop also criticized the skimpiness of the bathing attire the ordinary bathers were wearing on the beach.

177

Johnny Jack Nonus, according to Scharff. He said Johnny
Jack was the actual rumrunner, hiring the trucks and boats
and crews to get the liquor to the distributors. The people
handling the liquor sometimes were caught with it and they
sometimes talked. Johnny Jack went to Leavenworth four
times. George Musey went with him one time after the crews
of two boats seized at Seabrook did some talking. Musey
was shot to death at the corner of 25th Street and Market
one day shortly after he got out of prison.

The Maceo brothers lived longer lives and died of natural
causes. Scharff says he thought he had a conspiracy case
against the brothers once. The jury found them not guilty
after listening to prominent clergymen and others testify
about all the good deeds the Maceos had done.

Cotton broker Baylis E. Harriss was mayor in 1923.
Albert Farb was in the grocery business but about to move
to Houston. He went into real estate in Houston and his son,
Harold, joined the business in 1944.

The Diocese of Galveston-Houston bought the Walter

Opposite: *All other traffic on Seawall Boulevard stopped for the 1930 Cotton Carnival parade.*

Above: *Other amusement piers have come and gone over the years. Murdock's has been here at 23rd Street for generations. There was a ballroom, bingo parlor, cafe, gift shop, arcade and photo studio in addition to dressing rooms when this picture was made in the 1940s. A couple of fragments of this structure stand on the site today. A large part of the pier was wrecked by Hurricane Carla and never rebuilt.*

Gresham castle in 1923 to serve as a residence for the bishop. C.E. Byrne was bishop at the time. He lived in the house until he died in 1950.

W.L. Moody, Jr. bought the *Galveston News* from the A.H. Belo Company in 1923. He bought the *Galveston Tribune* in 1926. Moody continued to publish them as separate papers. Silas Ragsdale was editor of both. The United States National Bank completed a new building at Market and 22nd Street in 1924.

Top: *The Kempner's United States National Bank built a new building at Market and 22nd Street in 1924. This bank had earlier absorbed the Texas Bank and Trust Company, which had absorbed the Island City Savings Bank. United States National later merged with the Cullen-Frost bank holding company and that company was absorbed into the First City chain in 1983.*

Bottom: *The Moody family started what would become a very substantial chain of hotels in 1927 when Shearn Moody built the Jean Lafitte downtown on Church Street at 21st. The hotel was named for the privateer whose name usually is spelled Laffite.*

Opposite: *Shearn Moody built the Buccaneer Hotel on the seawall at 23rd Street in 1928. It was a fashionable resort for many years, but it was getting a little dowdy by the time the Moody Foundation gave it to the Methodist Church. It is a retirement home now, called Moody House.*

Jack E. Pearce was elected mayor in 1925. He served for ten years. The county started building a road up the Bolivar Peninsula. The ferry service established to carry cars across the channel entrance was taken over by the state highway department in 1933. The first paved road between Galveston and Houston was finished in 1928.

The Tremont Hotel was demolished in 1928. The demolition crew discovered in the attic an old guest register that visitors to the lookout tower had signed during the days when a vantage point six floors above the ground was something to be exclaimed over. Some of the names found in the register were Rutherford B. Hayes, U.S. Grant, Grover Cleveland, Benjamin Harrison, James Garfield, Chester A. Arthur, Edwin Booth, Porfirio Diaz, Chief Spotted Horse and Buffalo Bill Cody. Many of the visitors wrote comments about the great view. Some of the signatures may well be forgeries, but the register is preserved in the Rosenberg Library.

The Houston Ship Channel had been deepened to thirty

feet in 1925. There were eight refineries on the Houston channel. The Houston port had a new grain elevator and several cotton compresses. It was in the middle twenties that the Houston port began to surpass Galveston in total tonnage. There was some tendency in Galveston to shrug off the Houston statistics as "mostly liquid cargo." Houston had an advantage in competing for cotton shipments, too. It cost a little less to ship cotton to Houston from the interior by rail. E.H. Thornton of the Galveston Chamber of Commerce managed to get the railroad rates equalized so the freight rate for cotton to either port was the same. That helped. Galveston had twenty cotton compresses in 1928 with a storage capacity of one and a half million bales. Galveston was still the leading cotton port, but Houston was gaining.

Rice historian Earl W. Fornell wrote that Galveston lost its position as the greatest Texas seaport because short-sighted leaders followed a policy of profit-taking and conservative expansion at a time when trade and the competition from Houston were growing. Complacency may have had something to do with it, but it is not possible for anyone to say whether a different policy would have produced a different result. There was some public sentiment in 1928 in favor of the city taking over the wharves. Wharf Company president George Sealy, Jr. was opposed to it.

Galveston dropped to eighth place among Texas cities in 1930. The census of 1930 put the population at 52,938. Monsignor Daniel O'Connell was named rector of St. Mary's Cathedral. He served there until he died in 1966. O'Connell

Opposite: *The port of Houston was beginning to overtake the port of Galveston in the middle 1920s, but the Galveston port still had plenty of business. Mallory liners like the* Seminole *were making regular runs between Galveston and New York.*

Above: *Galveston was still the leading cotton port in the nation. Polyester hadn't been invented. The textile mills were buying tons of Texas cotton. Texas production was running between two and five million bales a year in the 1920s.*

was born in Ireland and ordained at the seminary in La Porte. The Bolivar Lighthouse was shut down in 1933. The lighthouse built in 1918 at the end of the south jetty served the harbor until 1983 when a beacon was installed on East Beach. Frank Biaggne was elected sheriff in 1933. He had been in the Merchant Marine and had been a fireman and a policeman before he ran for sheriff.

Weak beer became legal in 1933 when Congress modified the Volstead Act to permit beer with 3.2 percent alcoholic content.

The Galveston Buccaneers won the Texas League Baseball Championship in 1934, but lost to New Orleans in the Dixie Series. Shearn Moody owned the Buccaneers at the time. He died two years later.

Texans voted in August, 1935, to repeal the prohibition law adopted in 1918 and allow liquor to be sold in package stores on a local option basis. The federal prohibition amendment already had been repealed. The bootleggers' day was about done, but the gambling business was better than ever.

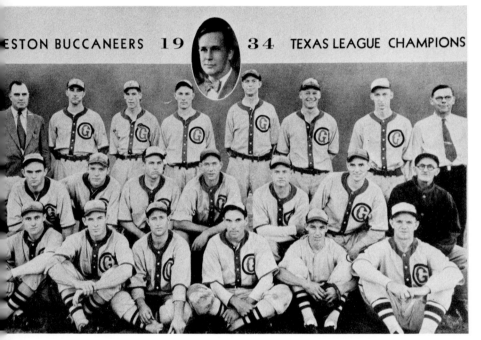

Top: *The Santa Fe Railroad completed an office building and depot on 25th Street at The Strand in 1932. The building was vacant for a long time after the railroad closed its Galveston offices in 1960. the Moody Foundation bought the building in 1976.*

Bottom: *Shearn Moody's Buccaneers won the Texas League baseball championship in 1934. Shearn, inset, seldom finished last in any endeavor. He was the Moody most people thought most likely to follow in the footsteps of his father and grandfather. He had inherited their acquisitiveness and knack for business, but he did not inherit the Moodys' durability. Shearn died young in 1936.*

Adrian Levy was elected mayor in 1935. The Galveston channel was deepened to thirty-six feet and work started on a series of groins to control erosion of the beach in front of the seawall. The seawall was eight miles long. It had been extended by three miles in 1921 and by another mile in 1926.

Galveston voters approved the creation of a junior college in 1935, but the creation was delayed for thirty-one years. Voters declined twice to approve a tax to pay for the college. The tax was not approved until 1966.

A new federal courthouse was completed in 1936 on the same site where the courthouse designed by Nicholas Clayton had stood.

Texans were showing a clear preference for traveling on their own wheels and the interurban made its last run to Houston October 31, 1936. Babe Harper was the conductor on the last trip.

The presidential yacht stopped at Galveston in 1937 to put President Franklin D. Roosevelt ashore. The President had been fishing for tarpon in the Gulf. He had a brief visit and then took a train to Fort Worth to see his son, Elliott. The younger Roosevelt was then running radio station KFJZ and the Texas State Network. Mayor Levy was beginning to talk about a bridge to Pelican Island by 1938. He also favored a bridge across the harbor entrance to Bolivar Point. That idea went to a vote and it was defeated. Mayor Levy happened to be in New York when that city put on a big reception for Douglas Corrigan. People had been getting killed trying to duplicate Lindberg's flight across the Atlantic. Federal authorities clamped down on the flights just before Douglas Corrigan planned to fly across the ocean. Corrigan pretended to accept the government edict. He announced he was taking off for California. Then he took off and flew to Ireland. He claimed he flew the wrong way by mistake. The newspapers called him "Wrong Way Corrigan." He was a hero. He had been born in Galveston. Mayor Levy invited him to come to Galveston for a reception.

Corrigan apparently did not enjoy his visit to the old hometown very much. He mentioned when he was presented

Opposite top: *The federal courthouse and post office building that still serves Galveston was built in 1936. The weather office is on the top floor. The dome on the roof covers the antenna for the radar set that helped make Dan Rather famous during Hurricane Carla in 1961. An earlier hurricane, in 1943, blew the roof off this building.*

Opposite center: *One of President Franklin Roosevelt's sons was living in Fort Worth in 1937. The president went fishing for tarpon in the Gulf that summer and came ashore at Galveston to take a train to Fort Worth. Mayor Adrian Levy, right, presided at the reception. Governor Jimmy Allred showed up with a young congressional candidate named Lyndon Johnson. It is plain from the*

expression on the mayor's face that he felt like Johnson crashed the party.

Opposite bottom: *Adrian Levy is one of the most gracious citizens Galveston ever produced but he had a disagreeable experience with another guest in 1938. The mayor staged a civic reception for Galveston native Douglas "Wrong Way" Corrigan after Corrigan flew the Atlantic. Southern Select beer helped sponsor the affair. Corrigan embarrassed his hosts by taking loud exception to the beer sponsorship. He said he did not like beer.*

a wristwatch at a luncheon that he already had several wristwatches. He was escorted to an apartment at 21st Street and Market. A plaque had been installed in one of the rooms proclaiming it to be the room where Corrigan was born. Corrigan disputed the information on the plaque and claimed that he was born in John Sealy Hospital. What excitement there was over his visit died down very quickly.

Brantley Harris was elected mayor in 1939 and served until he died in 1942. Harris initiated the development of Stewart Beach Park on the beach at Broadway and the Municipal Pleasure Pier over the Gulf.

Quadruplet daughters were born February 2, 1939, to the William E. Badgetts. The girls were named Jeraldine, Joan, Jeanette and Joyce. The city gave the Badgetts a house and the girls endured considerable publicity as they were growing up.

The highway department finished work on a new and wider causeway between the island and the mainland in 1939. Motor traffic was shifted to the new bridge, but trains

Above: *Fertility pills had not been invented in 1939 and multiple births were much less common than they are today. There was great excitement when Mrs. William E. Badgett gave birth to quadruplets at St. Mary's Hospital on February 2. The city saw in them another tourist attraction. The city and the Chamber of Commerce accordingly built the Badgetts a house in the 900 block of Broadway. The house where the Badgett girls grew up has recently been converted to an office building.*

Below: *The four little Badgetts made public appearances constantly and their pictures appeared regularly in the national press. The girls were named Joyce, Jeannette, Jeraldine and Joan. Two of them still live in Galveston. The other two live in Dallas. All four are married. They have thirteen children among them.*

Opposite: *The 1911 causeway was still the only link to the mainland when the first Burlington streamliner paid a visit to the island in 1934.*

continued to use the causeway built in 1911. The 1939 causeway was built with a lift bridge in the middle. Cars and trucks had to stop and wait when tugs were passing under the bridge. This awkward arrangement prevailed until a high bridge was built in 1961. Then the 1939 causeway was rebuilt to rise above the traffic in the canal. This is the bridge that now carries the traffic on the northbound side of I-45. The 1961 bridge carries the southbound freeway traffic.

The census of 1940 showed the population of Galveston had risen to 60,862. Seven Texas cities had more people. The city had a minority interest in the Wharf Company before 1940. Business was declining. The wharves needed expensive repairs. The majority owners let themselves be persuaded to sell out to the city. Merchant Harry Levy engineered an election. People voted $6.25 million worth of revenue bonds. The city gave the bonds to the Sealys and their associates and took over full ownership of the wharves. The deal specified that there would be a Wharves Board with five members. The former majority owners were allowed to name three of the members until the city redeemed $2.5 million worth of the revenue bonds. The old guard was really still in charge.

The Galveston Housing Authority was established in 1940 to build some housing for the poor. The authority started work on Oleander Homes and Palm Terrace, but the poor had to wait a while to move in. The projects were reserved before they were finished for the people brought in to work in the shipyards and on the military bases. The Pleasure Pier

Above: *The city of Galveston acquired full ownership of the wharves when Mayor Brantley Harris, left, handed Wharf Company president George Sealy, Jr. a check for $6,250,000 at this ceremony in 1940. The city did not get actual control of the wharves, though, until 1947.*

Below: *A new Kirwin Catholic High School was built in 1942 at 23rd Street and Avenue M, to replace the original school that stood on the same site. This site had previously been occupied by the late Colonel W.L. Moody's home. Kirwin was named for Monsignor James Kirwin, rector of St. Mary's Cathedral. It was a high school for boys until 1968 when it was consolidated with the Ursuline and Dominican girls' schools and re-named O'Connell High School for*

Monsignor Daniel O'Connell. The present school on the original Ursuline Academy campus is part of O'Connell High School, accommodating the seventh and eighth grades.

Opposite top: *World War II brought a big increase in the garrisons at the three forts protecting Galveston. The big guns at Fort Travis on Bolivar, Fort San Jacinto at the east end of the island and Fort Crockett on the seawall were manned around the clock. Two of the guns at Fort Crockett were twelve-inchers. The concussion when they were fired was something memorable. The Army started holding firing drills without notice. There were so many complaints that the gunners reluctantly started giving the citizens advance notice.*

the city built with $2 million borrowed from the government was completed just in time to be taken over by the Army for the duration of World War II. The Air Corps used the buildings on the pier for storage. The Army Air Corps also established a base at Municipal Airport and called it Scholes Field. Fort Crockett was expanded. The Army moved 2,500 men in to man the guns there, at Fort San Jacinto on the eastern end of the island and at Fort Travis on Bolivar Point. The forts had some ten- and-twelve-inch guns and batteries of anti-aircraft guns. The Germans never attacked, but the soldiers fired the big guns for drill occasionally and broke some of the neighbors' windows. Todd Shipbuilding had taken over the docks and yards developed by the Galveston Dry Dock and Construction Company in 1934. The Todd drydocks on Pelican Island were expanded during the war to handle warships. The first practice blackout the night of January 7, 1942, was pronounced a success. The city was completely blacked out only for drills, but lights were banned within three blocks of the beach.

Below: *The Galveston airport was turned into a base for Army patrol bombers during World War II. A few of the buildings the Army built are still standing. German U-boats were sinking ships in the Gulf regularly during the first two years of the war in spite of the Army's patrol bombers and the blimps the Navy operated from Hitchcock.*

Navy blimps based at Hitchcock and Army bombers based at Scholes Field patrolled the Gulf, but German submarines sank many ships. Tankers were special targets. Some Galvestonians can remember seeing the glow of burning ships on the night horizon, as many as four in one night. The submarine menace was what prompted the building of the pipelines to carry petroleum products from Texas to the East Coast.

Mayor Brantley Harris died in 1942. Henry Flagg won a special election and then lost to George Fraser in the regular election in 1943.

The Navy gave the city's name to one of the new cruisers built during the war. Mrs. Clark Thompson christened the U.S.S. *Galveston* at the shipyard in Philadelphia. She promised that she and Thompson would give a party for the crew the first time the ship visited Galveston. The cruiser went into mothballs for a while after the war and it was 1960 before she made it to Galveston. Congressman and Mrs. Thompson put on a party in Moody Center.

Maco Stewart and the Sealy and Hutchings estates liquidated the old Galveston City Company during the war. The Army moved out of the buildings on the Pleasure Pier after the war ended. The dance pavilion, the midway and the fishing pier were opened to the public in 1946. The idea had been borrowed from Atlantic City, but the attractions on the pier never drew the crowds the city had hoped for. The carriage trade went to the Balinese Room. Young families went to the beach. Galveston never had much in common with Atlantic City.

Herbert Cartwright, Jr. was elected mayor in 1947. He was perfectly comfortable with Galveston's reputation as an open city, but it bothered him that the former owners of the wharves still had control after selling out to the city. Cartwright promoted another election. He got a new bond issue approved to redeem the revenue bonds the city had issued to the wharf owners. W.L. Moody, Jr. bought the new bond issue.The city got control of the wharves.

Ships were getting bigger and the Galveston channel was

Opposite: *The Todd Shipyard on Pelican Island expanded during the war to handle repairs to damaged warships and merchantmen. The work force at Todd grew from 900 before the war started to nearly 5,000 at the height of the war.*

Above: *The school district built a new building for Ball High School in 1953 on a vastly bigger campus on Avenue O at 41st Street.*

deepened to thirty-eight feet in 1948. The Texas section of the Intracoastal Waterway was completed in 1949. This protected canal parallels the coast from Brownsville to Florida. It is used mostly by tugs and barges.

The Wharves Board had persuaded E.H. Thornton to give up his job at the Port of New Orleans to take over management of the Galveston wharves. Thornton made improvements and brought some of the port's business back. The port had a setback in the 1950s when the federal government accused the elevators of mixing damaged grain with good grain being shipped abroad. This cost the port some grain business, but the federal inquiry eventually turned up evidence that Galveston was not the only port that had been careless with grain.

Several other Texas cities were growing faster than Galveston right after the war. The census of 1950 showed twelve Texas cities with more population than Galveston's 65,898.

A controversy developed in 1950 over a plan to widen Broadway. There were no longer any interurbans or streetcars running down the esplanade. The automobile traffic on the roadways had increased beyond anything the original planners imagined. The city wanted to cut the esplanade down to add another lane to the roadway on each side. Many people wanted to keep the wide esplanade.There was a referendum. The plan to widen the roadways carried by just sixty-three votes. The landscaping on the esplanade was redone. The reduced esplanade is still wider than most.

Maco Stewart Jr. died in 1950. He left a will giving his wife and two sons a life interest in his Galveston Island ranch and providing that the ranch should eventually pass to the state to become a park.

The Gulf Freeway between Houston and Galveston was completed in 1952.

W.L. Moody, Jr. died in 1954 leaving the bulk of his great fortune to the Moody Foundation and leaving his daughter, Mary, in charge of most of his enterprises. W.L. Moody III got one dollar in his father's will. He sued the estate. He claimed he was at least entitled to a share of the estate his

194

mother left when she died in 1943. Moody III won a settlement of $3.5 million. His sister, Libbie Moody Thompson, sued for a share of the mother's estate, too. She also won a settlement. The settlements did not bankrupt the Moody Foundation. It was reported at the time to be the third richest foundation in the country. Only the Rockefeller and Ford foundations were believed to be bigger. The trustees of the foundation in the beginning were Mary Moody Northen, W.L. Moody IV and Shearn Moody's sons, Robert and Shearn, Jr.

George Clough was elected mayor in 1955. Galveston ceased to be an open city during his administration, but it was not because of anything Clough did.

Paul Hopkins was elected sheriff in 1956.

The Moody interests built the Moody Convention Center on the seawall at 22nd Street in 1957.

The Galveston Progress Committee decided that the city might attract a little favorable attention if somebody flew a single-engine airplane to Rome without stopping. The

His American National Insurance Company had outgrown the first building he built for it and was occupying this building at 21st and Mechanic by the time W.L. Moody, Jr. died in 1954. This building had originally been called the Medical Arts Building.

Top: *The First Lady of Galveston. Mary Moody Northen was sixty-two the year she succeeded her father as president of the American National Insurance Company and head of the Moody empire.*

Bottom: *Galveston is served by two radio stations. KGBC went on the air in 1947. The present studio and transmitter are on Pelican Island.*

Opposite top: *KILE is older. It was established in 1928 by the late mayor George Clough's family. The call letters were changed when the station changed hands in the late 1950s. The original call letters were KLUF.*

committee offered a prize of $1,000. Bill Wyat took off from Galveston in 1957 in a Mooney monoplane and he almost made it. He climbed so high trying to get above a thunderstorm off the coast of Spain that his wings iced up and he had to make a crash landing in the sea. Wyatt survived. The Galveston committee decided it was a good faith effort and gave him the prize.

Below: *Galveston had a television station once. Paul Taft and others established Channel 11 on the island in 1953. The station was originally called KGUL-TV. The studio was at 45th Street and Avenue P½. This section of P½ was renamed Video Lane when the station opened. Channel 11 moved to Houston in 1958 and the call letters were changed to KHOU-TV. The Group W cable system moved into the old studio on Video Lane in 1983.*

PART FIVE

After Will Wilson 1957-1983

Will Wilson told the Galveston Rotarians in 1957 that Galveston should develop something like Disneyland to draw the family trade. He said a family in a station wagon would leave more money in Galveston than a gambler would. Galvestonians had long complained, though, that the families from Houston brought all their food and drinks with them and left nothing but trash behind.

Galveston and Galveston County have collected lots of taxes from Houstonians since 1957. There were a few farms and ranches and summer houses on the west end of the island before. The development of resort subdivisions started in 1957. Sea Isle was the original subdivision. David Feinman was offering lots there for $15 a month in the spring of '57. Johnny Goyen and Earl Galceran started the Jamaica Beach Subdivision later the same year. Their prices started at $1,250. Big lots fronting the beach were $3,500. Most of the buyers were Houstonians.

The government decided to dispose of the forts on the island and started selling off parts of Fort Crockett in 1957.

The attorney general got interested in the Moody Foundation after he closed the Galveston gambling houses. Wilson filed a court suit alleging that the people of Texas were being deprived of the benefits of the charitable trust because the four Moody Foundation trustees could not agree on anything. Wilson claimed that Mrs. Northen and W.L. Moody IV voted together and Robert and Shearn, Jr. voted against them and the board was deadlocked most of the time.

The bridge from Galveston to Pelican Island was finished in February, 1958. It cost $6 million. A bond issue was

The jetties at the Bolivar ferry landing are popular fishing spots, and free.

voted to pay for it. The city had sold most of the undeveloped land on the island to Merritt, Chapman and Scott of New York by this time. The New Yorkers spent several million dollars filling and improving the island and then sold out in 1962 to George Mitchell. Houston oilman Bob Smith acquired the yacht basin near Fort Point in 1958. He was devoted to fishing much more than to yachting, but he said he wanted to make the Galveston yacht anchorage the equal of anything anywhere. He did.

Top: *Environmentalists have slowed development down considerably, but developers in the 1960s were dredging canals on the west end of Galveston Island and creating waterfront subdivisions. Sea Isle was the first substantial one.*

Bottom: *Johnny Goyen and his partners developed Jamaica Beach as a retreat for Houstonians. The builders put up basic houses in the beginning, but the homes grew more and more elaborate as the memory of Hurricane Carla receded.*

The real estate developers on the west end started putting up bathhouses on the beach and fences to keep cars off the beaches adjacent to their developments. This stirred up the legislature and Will Wilson. The beaches in Texas are public property. Nobody has the right to exclude anybody else from any section of the beach. Some people believe they have a constitutional right to drive on the beach. Several sunbathers have been run over by drivers exercising this alleged right. The legislature passed a new bill in 1959 guaranteeing public access to the beaches. Wilson started litigating to get the fences taken down. No part of Texas got more attention than Galveston when Will Wilson was attorney general.

Herbert Cartwright defeated George Clough and returned to the mayor's office in 1959. The attorney general's complaint against the Moody Foundation board was resolved with the appointment of three new trustees from outside the Moody family. They were J.S. Leach, the retired chairman of Texaco; J.M.Lykes, Jr. of the steamship family; and

Homes worth hundreds of thousands of dollars were being built at Pirates' Beach and other west end subdivisions shortly before Hurricane Alicia struck in 1983.

S.M. Greer, chairman of the First City National Bank.

There was an election in 1960 to change the form of the city government. It was brought on by a campaign to restore the mayor-council form. Mayor Cartwright was for keeping the commission form. One of the leaders of the movement advocating a change was merchant Eddie Schreiber. His side prevailed. The new city council chose Schreiber to be mayor. The census of 1960 put the population at 67,175. Galveston had slipped to fifteenth place among Texas cities.

Top: *The late Houston oil millionaire R.E. "Bob" Smith, right was an enthusiastic fisherman. He often went fishing off Galveston with George Mitchell, left, and Charlie Wuest and he wasn't satisfied with the place he had to keep his boat.*

Bottom: *Smith swapped some land he owned at Mykawa for a piece of harbor front property near the U.T. Medical Branch. Millions of dollars' worth of yachts are berthed now in the yacht basin Bob Smith built.*

Left: *The black civil rights campaign never generated the kind of heat in Galveston that it generated in some other Southern cities. Merchants and business leaders started talking about desegregating immediately after Kelton Sams and a group of black high school students staged a sit-in at Woolworth's lunch counter. George Clampett's Star Drug Store was the first to begin serving blacks. The other lunch counters followed suit. The schools would have been desegregated earlier than they were if the state legislature had not passed a law denying state money to integrated school systems.*

Right: *Texans have long believed they should be entitled to drive their cars, RVs and motorcycles on any beach. But Galveston and Galveston County have recently developed several parks where cars are restricted to parking areas.*

The racial tension that characterized the civil rights movement of the 1960s in some other Southern cities was largely absent in Galveston. The city had some ghettos and it has some still. There were separate schools, but blacks and whites had lived in fairly close proximity to each other from the beginning. Slaves lived on the owners' property. Servants lived on their employers' property after slavery ended. Some very modest houses were built adjacent to mansions when the big lots were subdivided. Some of the modest houses were occupied by black people. Mixed neighborhoods were more the rule than the exception long before the sixties. The schools were desegregated without the confrontations some other communities witnessed.

The Galveston Marine Aquarium Corporation, headed by J.N. Dismukes of Austin, bought fifty-four acres on the seawall in 1960 and announced plans for Searama Marine Park.

District Judge L.D. Goddard gave the attorney general in 1961 the order he wanted requiring developers to remove fences and barricades from the beaches. Municipalities were later empowered to fence out motor vehicles. There are barricades at each end of the beach in Galveston Island State Park and motor vehicles are barred from the beaches in city and county parks. But they are a serious hazard on much of the beach still.

The Weather Bureau had some radar stations by 1961, and airplanes capable of flying into hurricanes and many more observation stations than before. The weathermen could issue earlier warnings, but they were no more certain where a hurricane would go than they had ever been. Ernest Carson was the man in charge at the Galveston Weather Office. The Weather Bureau had adopted a custom of naming hurricanes in 1952. The storm that blew up in the West Indies in early September, 1961, was named Carla. The storm became a hurricane on September 6 and entered the Gulf of Mexico September 7.

Residents of most other coastal cities were moving inland by September 9. Galvestonians felt more secure behind their seawall. No more than about fifteen percent of the city's population moved to the mainland, but all the west end of the island was evacuated.

The storm stalled off the coast September 10 and then crashed ashore on the eleventh near Port O'Connor, 100 miles west of Galveston. Indianola would have been right in Carla's path if Indianola had not been wiped out in 1886. The winds at the center of the storm were probably 175 miles an hour. Galveston had gusts up to 117 miles an hour and tides ten feet above normal — and that was just the edge

Right: *Galveston did not have a really destructive hurricane between 1943 and 1961. Hurricanes were being given names by 1961 and the third hurricane of that season was called Carla. The main force of Carla actually struck near Port O'Connor September 11, but Galveston suffered destructive winds and tides.*

Below: *The greatest damage in the city proper was caused by a tornado that spun out of the storm and cut a path across the island from the beach to the port. Dozens of buildings were demolished.*

Carla was the largest hurricane ever recorded. It hovered off the coast and threatened Galveston for hours before it finally moved to the west. Dan Rather of Channel 11 spent those anxious hours in the Galveston weather office reporting to his station and CBS what the weathermen were learning from the radar pictures. Rather was talking with weatherman Vaughn Rockney when this photograph was made from a television screen.

of the storm. A tornado spun out of the disintegrating storm early on the morning of the twelfth. It hit the Pleasure Pier on the seawall at 23rd Street and cut right across the island to the docks. The tornado destroyed most of the buildings in a strip four blocks wide and twenty blocks long. The county courthouse that caused Nicholas Clayton so much grief was damaged badly. The city withstood the hurricane well. Most of the damage was done by the tornado. It killed seven people.

Galveston was isolated during the storm. The freeway was under water. The ferries stopped running. No planes could fly. But there was some phone service throughout the emergency. The *Galveston News* and *Tribune* missed a couple of editions because of power failure. Galveston Radio Station KGBC managed to stay on the air with an emergency generator. Channel 11 had moved its headquarters from Galveston to Houston in 1958, but the station still had a studio in Galveston and a line from there to the transmitter at Alvin. Channel 11 News Director Dan Rather became a national celebrity during the storm with his live reports from the Galveston Weather Bureau to KHOU-TV and CBS. Channel 2's Tom Jarriel made a film record of the storm that is still the best hurricane film in existence.

Many newsmen stayed in the Buccaneer Hotel on the seawall during the storm. The sturdy hotel was a safe haven and also a splendid vantage point. There may never be that much excitement there again. The Moody Foundation gave the hotel to the Texas Conference of Methodist Churches three months after the storm passed. It was converted to a retirement home.

The city council surprised Eddie Schreiber in 1962 by choosing Councilman Ted Stubbs to replace him as mayor. Houston banker James Lyon leased the Pleasure Pier and built the Flagship Hotel on it. Carla had done some damage to the buildings on the pier but none to the pier itself. The storm did major damage to the nearby Murdock's Pier and the Balinese Room.

Falstaff opened a new brewery ·in 1962. The Texas

The Falstaff Brewing Company bought out the old Galveston Brewery in 1956. Falstaff enlarged and modernized the plant in 1962 and then sold it to the owners of the Pearl Brewery in 1975. The Pearl people closed this brewery in 1979. No beer is now brewed in Galveston.

Maritime Academy was established the same year. Another extension of the seawall was completed. The extension gave the wall a total length of 10.4 miles. About two thirds of the island remains unprotected. There has been no talk about extending the wall farther.

The expanded board of trustees of the Moody Foundation decided in August, 1962, to offer the *Galveston News* and the *Galveston Tribune* for sale. Mary Moody Northen said it was a mistake and subsequent events proved she was right.

Oveta Hobby bought the Galveston papers. She owned the *Houston Post*. Her approach to serving the readers of Texas' oldest newspaper was to give them something different. She abandoned the most historic newspaper building in Texas. She built a new plant next to the causeway where it could also print her Texas City newspaper. The *Galveston News* had been a morning paper. Mrs. Hobby merged it with the *Tribune*. She continued to call it the *Galveston News,* but it became an afternoon paper Monday through Friday.

Opposite top: *The* Galveston News *and* Galveston Tribune *passed out of local hands in 1962. The publisher of the* Houston Post *bought the papers and upset a lot of Galvestonians by combining them into one paper called the* Galveston Daily News *even though it came out only six days a week. The* Post *publisher built the present publishing plant near the causeway and sold it in 1967.*

Opposite center: *The Todd Company won the contract for servicing the experimental nuclear merchant ship* Savannah *in 1960. One of the docks at the Todd yard on Pelican Island was rebuilt to handle the sleek ship. She made several stops here before she was taken out of service in 1971. Some Galvestonians wanted to keep the* Savannah *here as a tourist attraction. The port of Savannah made a more persuasive argument, but the ship was later moved from Savannah to Charleston. She is now open to visitors there.*

Opposite bottom: *The Moody Foundation gave the Moody Convention Center on the seawall to the city in 1964. The center was buttoned up for Hurricane Alicia when this picture was made. It suffered some damage as most buildings on the seawall did.*

There was a Sunday morning edition but no edition on Saturday. Galvestonians thought she was trying to sell them the *Houston Post*. They showed little enthusiasm for the changes. Mrs. Hobby sold the paper in 1967 to Galveston Newspapers, Inc. Les Daughtry became publisher. The *Galveston News* became a morning paper again and resumed publishing on Saturdays.

Eddie Schreiber returned to the mayor's office in 1963. The Todd Shipyard on Pelican Island became the service port for the nuclear merchant ship *Savannah*. The *Savannah* was refueled here in 1968 and then defueled here in 1971 when she was taken out of service and moved to the port of Savannah.

The Flagship Hotel opened on the old Pleasure Pier in 1965. Several large motels had been built on the beachfront in the meantime, but the Flagship was the first major new hotel on the beach in thirty-seven years.

The county commissioners decided to demolish and replace the old courthouse damaged by Carla. Stewart Title Company president Stewart Morris bought the old granite columns. He gave some of them to Houston Baptist University in Houston and installed the others at the entrance to the Sugar Creek subdivision in Sugar Land. Stewart Morris and his brother, Carloss, are nephews of the Stewart Title founder.

Galveston got another connection to the mainland in 1966. The county completed work on the Vacek bridge over San Luis Pass completing a highway link between Galveston and Freeport.

Opposite: *Houston banker James Lyon made a deal to lease the old Galveston Pleasure Pier in 1962. He built the Flagship Hotel and it has been advertised ever since it opened in 1965 as the only hotel in the country built over tide water. The Flagship suffered some damage during Hurricane Alicia, but the concrete pier was unscathed.*

Above: *Galveston County got a new courthouse in 1965. The county commissioners decided to tear down the courthouse damaged by Carla. They put up this building on the same site on 21st Street between Winnie and Ball.*

Houston architect Howard Barnstone ruffled some Galveston feathers in 1966 when he published his book on Galveston architecture. The city's decline in population and importance and the corresponding decline in the economic base were reflected in the city's facade. A few of the great palaces had been kept up, but handsome old homes and commercial buildings were decaying on every hand. Barnstone's book and the photographs by Henri Cartier-Bresson and Ezra Stoller called more attention to the decay than some Galvestonians thought seemly. Some believe, though, that *The Galveston That Was* helped kindle the present interest in restoring and preserving Galveston's remaining architectural treasures.

Galveston College opened in 1967 in the old St. Mary's Orphanage building at 41st Street and Avenue Q.

The population of Galveston had stopped growing. The census of 1970 put the figure at 61,809. Galveston was the twentieth city in the state until the next census. The census of 1980 produced a total of 61,902. Galveston had slipped

PART FIVE

After Will Wilson 1957-1983

Will Wilson told the Galveston Rotarians in 1957 that Galveston should develop something like Disneyland to draw the family trade. He said a family in a station wagon would leave more money in Galveston than a gambler would. Galvestonians had long complained, though, that the families from Houston brought all their food and drinks with them and left nothing but trash behind.

Galveston and Galveston County have collected lots of taxes from Houstonians since 1957. There were a few farms and ranches and summer houses on the west end of the island before. The development of resort subdivisions started in 1957. Sea Isle was the original subdivision. David Feinman was offering lots there for $15 a month in the spring of '57. Johnny Goyen and Earl Galceran started the Jamaica Beach Subdivision later the same year. Their prices started at $1,250. Big lots fronting the beach were $3,500. Most of the buyers were Houstonians.

The government decided to dispose of the forts on the island and started selling off parts of Fort Crockett in 1957.

The attorney general got interested in the Moody Foundation after he closed the Galveston gambling houses. Wilson filed a court suit alleging that the people of Texas were being deprived of the benefits of the charitable trust because the four Moody Foundation trustees could not agree on anything. Wilson claimed that Mrs. Northen and W.L. Moody IV voted together and Robert and Shearn, Jr. voted against them and the board was deadlocked most of the time.

The bridge from Galveston to Pelican Island was finished in February, 1958. It cost $6 million. A bond issue was

The jetties at the Bolivar ferry landing are popular fishing spots, and free.

voted to pay for it. The city had sold most of the undeveloped land on the island to Merritt, Chapman and Scott of New York by this time. The New Yorkers spent several million dollars filling and improving the island and then sold out in 1962 to George Mitchell. Houston oilman Bob Smith acquired the yacht basin near Fort Point in 1958. He was devoted to fishing much more than to yachting, but he said he wanted to make the Galveston yacht anchorage the equal of anything anywhere. He did.

Top: *Environmentalists have slowed development down considerably, but developers in the 1960s were dredging canals on the west end of Galveston Island and creating waterfront subdivisions. Sea Isle was the first substantial one.*

Bottom: *Johnny Goyen and his partners developed Jamaica Beach as a retreat for Houstonians. The builders put up basic houses in the beginning, but the homes grew more and more elaborate as the memory of Hurricane Carla receded.*

The real estate developers on the west end started putting up bathhouses on the beach and fences to keep cars off the beaches adjacent to their developments. This stirred up the legislature and Will Wilson. The beaches in Texas are public property. Nobody has the right to exclude anybody else from any section of the beach. Some people believe they have a constitutional right to drive on the beach. Several sunbathers have been run over by drivers exercising this alleged right. The legislature passed a new bill in 1959 guaranteeing public access to the beaches. Wilson started litigating to get the fences taken down. No part of Texas got more attention than Galveston when Will Wilson was attorney general.

Herbert Cartwright defeated George Clough and returned to the mayor's office in 1959. The attorney general's complaint against the Moody Foundation board was resolved with the appointment of three new trustees from outside the Moody family. They were J.S. Leach, the retired chairman of Texaco; J.M.Lykes, Jr. of the steamship family; and

Homes worth hundreds of thousands of dollars were being built at Pirates' Beach and other west end subdivisions shortly before Hurricane Alicia struck in 1983.

S.M. Greer, chairman of the First City National Bank.

There was an election in 1960 to change the form of the city government. It was brought on by a campaign to restore the mayor-council form. Mayor Cartwright was for keeping the commission form. One of the leaders of the movement advocating a change was merchant Eddie Schreiber. His side prevailed. The new city council chose Schreiber to be mayor. The census of 1960 put the population at 67,175. Galveston had slipped to fifteenth place among Texas cities.

Top: *The late Houston oil millionaire R.E. "Bob" Smith, right was an enthusiastic fisherman. He often went fishing off Galveston with George Mitchell, left, and Charlie Wuest and he wasn't satisfied with the place he had to keep his boat.*

Bottom: *Smith swapped some land he owned at Mykawa for a piece of harbor front property near the U.T. Medical Branch. Millions of dollars' worth of yachts are berthed now in the yacht basin Bob Smith built.*

Left: *The black civil rights campaign never generated the kind of heat in Galveston that it generated in some other Southern cities. Merchants and business leaders started talking about desegregating immediately after Kelton Sams and a group of black high school students staged a sit-in at Woolworth's lunch counter. George Clampett's Star Drug Store was the first to begin serving blacks. The other lunch counters followed suit. The schools would have been desegregated earlier than they were if the state legislature had not passed a law denying state money to integrated school systems.*

Right: *Texans have long believed they should be entitled to drive their cars, RVs and motorcycles on any beach. But Galveston and Galveston County have recently developed several parks where cars are restricted to parking areas.*

205

The racial tension that characterized the civil rights movement of the 1960s in some other Southern cities was largely absent in Galveston. The city had some ghettos and it has some still. There were separate schools, but blacks and whites had lived in fairly close proximity to each other from the beginning. Slaves lived on the owners' property. Servants lived on their employers' property after slavery ended. Some very modest houses were built adjacent to mansions when the big lots were subdivided. Some of the modest houses were occupied by black people. Mixed neighborhoods were more the rule than the exception long before the sixties. The schools were desegregated without the confrontations some other communities witnessed.

The Galveston Marine Aquarium Corporation, headed by J.N. Dismukes of Austin, bought fifty-four acres on the seawall in 1960 and announced plans for Searama Marine Park.

District Judge L.D. Goddard gave the attorney general in 1961 the order he wanted requiring developers to remove fences and barricades from the beaches. Municipalities were later empowered to fence out motor vehicles. There are barricades at each end of the beach in Galveston Island State Park and motor vehicles are barred from the beaches in city and county parks. But they are a serious hazard on much of the beach still.

The Weather Bureau had some radar stations by 1961, and airplanes capable of flying into hurricanes and many more observation stations than before. The weathermen could issue earlier warnings, but they were no more certain where a hurricane would go than they had ever been. Ernest Carson was the man in charge at the Galveston Weather Office. The Weather Bureau had adopted a custom of naming hurricanes in 1952. The storm that blew up in the West Indies in early September, 1961, was named Carla. The storm became a hurricane on September 6 and entered the Gulf of Mexico September 7.

Residents of most other coastal cities were moving inland by September 9. Galvestonians felt more secure behind their seawall. No more than about fifteen percent of the city's population moved to the mainland, but all the west end of the island was evacuated.

The storm stalled off the coast September 10 and then crashed ashore on the eleventh near Port O'Connor, 100 miles west of Galveston. Indianola would have been right in Carla's path if Indianola had not been wiped out in 1886. The winds at the center of the storm were probably 175 miles an hour. Galveston had gusts up to 117 miles an hour and tides ten feet above normal — and that was just the edge

Right: *Galveston did not have a really destructive hurricane between 1943 and 1961. Hurricanes were being given names by 1961 and the third hurricane of that season was called Carla. The main force of Carla actually struck near Port O'Connor September 11, but Galveston suffered destructive winds and tides.*

Below: *The greatest damage in the city proper was caused by a tornado that spun out of the storm and cut a path across the island from the beach to the port. Dozens of buildings were demolished.*

Carla was the largest hurricane ever recorded. It hovered off the coast and threatened Galveston for hours before it finally moved to the west. Dan Rather of Channel 11 spent those anxious hours in the Galveston weather office reporting to his station and CBS what the weathermen were learning from the radar pictures. Rather was talking with weatherman Vaughn Rockney when this photograph was made from a television screen.

of the storm. A tornado spun out of the disintegrating storm early on the morning of the twelfth. It hit the Pleasure Pier on the seawall at 23rd Street and cut right across the island to the docks. The tornado destroyed most of the buildings in a strip four blocks wide and twenty blocks long. The county courthouse that caused Nicholas Clayton so much grief was damaged badly. The city withstood the hurricane well. Most of the damage was done by the tornado. It killed seven people.

Galveston was isolated during the storm. The freeway was under water. The ferries stopped running. No planes could fly. But there was some phone service throughout the emergency. The *Galveston News* and *Tribune* missed a couple of editions because of power failure. Galveston Radio Station KGBC managed to stay on the air with an emergency generator. Channel 11 had moved its headquarters from Galveston to Houston in 1958, but the station still had a studio in Galveston and a line from there to the transmitter at Alvin. Channel 11 News Director Dan Rather became a national celebrity during the storm with his live reports from the Galveston Weather Bureau to KHOU-TV and CBS. Channel 2's Tom Jarriel made a film record of the storm that is still the best hurricane film in existence.

Many newsmen stayed in the Buccaneer Hotel on the seawall during the storm. The sturdy hotel was a safe haven and also a splendid vantage point. There may never be that much excitement there again. The Moody Foundation gave the hotel to the Texas Conference of Methodist Churches three months after the storm passed. It was converted to a retirement home.

The city council surprised Eddie Schreiber in 1962 by choosing Councilman Ted Stubbs to replace him as mayor. Houston banker James Lyon leased the Pleasure Pier and built the Flagship Hotel on it. Carla had done some damage to the buildings on the pier but none to the pier itself. The storm did major damage to the nearby Murdock's Pier and the Balinese Room.

Falstaff opened a new brewery ·in 1962. The Texas

The Falstaff Brewing Company bought out the old Galveston Brewery in 1956. Falstaff enlarged and modernized the plant in 1962 and then sold it to the owners of the Pearl Brewery in 1975. The Pearl people closed this brewery in 1979. No beer is now brewed in Galveston.

Maritime Academy was established the same year. Another extension of the seawall was completed. The extension gave the wall a total length of 10.4 miles. About two thirds of the island remains unprotected. There has been no talk about extending the wall farther.

The expanded board of trustees of the Moody Foundation decided in August, 1962, to offer the *Galveston News* and the *Galveston Tribune* for sale. Mary Moody Northen said it was a mistake and subsequent events proved she was right.

Oveta Hobby bought the Galveston papers. She owned the *Houston Post*. Her approach to serving the readers of Texas' oldest newspaper was to give them something different. She abandoned the most historic newspaper building in Texas. She built a new plant next to the causeway where it could also print her Texas City newspaper. The *Galveston News* had been a morning paper. Mrs. Hobby merged it with the *Tribune*. She continued to call it the *Galveston News,* but it became an afternoon paper Monday through Friday.

Opposite top: *The* Galveston News *and* Galveston Tribune *passed out of local hands in 1962. The publisher of the* Houston Post *bought the papers and upset a lot of Galvestonians by combining them into one paper called the* Galveston Daily News *even though it came out only six days a week. The* Post *publisher built the present publishing plant near the causeway and sold it in 1967.*

Opposite center: *The Todd Company won the contract for servicing the experimental nuclear merchant ship* Savannah *in 1960. One of the docks at the Todd yard on Pelican Island was rebuilt to handle the sleek ship. She made several stops here before she was taken out of service in 1971. Some Galvestonians wanted to keep the* Savannah *here as a tourist attraction. The port of Savannah made a more persuasive argument, but the ship was later moved from Savannah to Charleston. She is now open to visitors there.*

Opposite bottom: *The Moody Foundation gave the Moody Convention Center on the seawall to the city in 1964. The center was buttoned up for Hurricane Alicia when this picture was made. It suffered some damage as most buildings on the seawall did.*

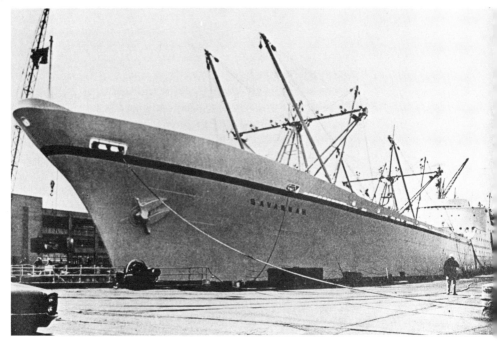

There was a Sunday morning edition but no edition on Saturday. Galvestonians thought she was trying to sell them the *Houston Post*. They showed little enthusiasm for the changes. Mrs. Hobby sold the paper in 1967 to Galveston Newspapers, Inc. Les Daughtry became publisher. The *Galveston News* became a morning paper again and resumed publishing on Saturdays.

Eddie Schreiber returned to the mayor's office in 1963. The Todd Shipyard on Pelican Island became the service port for the nuclear merchant ship *Savannah*. The *Savannah* was refueled here in 1968 and then defueled here in 1971 when she was taken out of service and moved to the port of Savannah.

The Flagship Hotel opened on the old Pleasure Pier in 1965. Several large motels had been built on the beachfront in the meantime, but the Flagship was the first major new hotel on the beach in thirty-seven years.

The county commissioners decided to demolish and replace the old courthouse damaged by Carla. Stewart Title Company president Stewart Morris bought the old granite columns. He gave some of them to Houston Baptist University in Houston and installed the others at the entrance to the Sugar Creek subdivision in Sugar Land. Stewart Morris and his brother, Carloss, are nephews of the Stewart Title founder.

Galveston got another connection to the mainland in 1966. The county completed work on the Vacek bridge over San Luis Pass completing a highway link between Galveston and Freeport.

There was a Sunday morning edition but no edition on Saturday. Galvestonians thought she was trying to sell them the *Houston Post*. They showed little enthusiasm for the changes. Mrs. Hobby sold the paper in 1967 to Galveston Newspapers, Inc. Les Daughtry became publisher. The *Galveston News* became a morning paper again and resumed publishing on Saturdays.

Eddie Schreiber returned to the mayor's office in 1963. The Todd Shipyard on Pelican Island became the service port for the nuclear merchant ship *Savannah*. The *Savannah* was refueled here in 1968 and then defueled here in 1971 when she was taken out of service and moved to the port of Savannah.

The Flagship Hotel opened on the old Pleasure Pier in 1965. Several large motels had been built on the beachfront in the meantime, but the Flagship was the first major new hotel on the beach in thirty-seven years.

The county commissioners decided to demolish and replace the old courthouse damaged by Carla. Stewart Title Company president Stewart Morris bought the old granite columns. He gave some of them to Houston Baptist University in Houston and installed the others at the entrance to the Sugar Creek subdivision in Sugar Land. Stewart Morris and his brother, Carloss, are nephews of the Stewart Title founder.

Galveston got another connection to the mainland in 1966. The county completed work on the Vacek bridge over San Luis Pass completing a highway link between Galveston and Freeport.

Opposite: *Houston banker James Lyon made a deal to lease the old Galveston Pleasure Pier in 1962. He built the Flagship Hotel and it has been advertised ever since it opened in 1965 as the only hotel in the country built over tide water. The Flagship suffered some damage during Hurricane Alicia, but the concrete pier was unscathed.*

Above: *Galveston County got a new courthouse in 1965. The county commissioners decided to tear down the courthouse damaged by Carla. They put up this building on the same site on 21st Street between Winnie and Ball.*

Houston architect Howard Barnstone ruffled some Galveston feathers in 1966 when he published his book on Galveston architecture. The city's decline in population and importance and the corresponding decline in the economic base were reflected in the city's facade. A few of the great palaces had been kept up, but handsome old homes and commercial buildings were decaying on every hand. Barnstone's book and the photographs by Henri Cartier-Bresson and Ezra Stoller called more attention to the decay than some Galvestonians thought seemly. Some believe, though, that *The Galveston That Was* helped kindle the present interest in restoring and preserving Galveston's remaining architectural treasures.

Galveston College opened in 1967 in the old St. Mary's Orphanage building at 41st Street and Avenue Q.

The population of Galveston had stopped growing. The census of 1970 put the figure at 61,809. Galveston was the twentieth city in the state until the next census. The census of 1980 produced a total of 61,902. Galveston had slipped

in 100 years from first place to thirty-first place among Texas cities. One reason was that increasing numbers of people employed in Galveston chose to live on the mainland in cities like Dickinson, Texas City and La Marque. Realtors said it was because there were few places for middle-class workers to live in Galveston. The city had numerous public housing projects for the very poor and plenty of decaying mansions only the rich could afford to buy and renovate. Developers have been building large apartment complexes

Opposite top: *The island got another link with the mainland in 1966 when the county completed the Vacek toll bridge over San Luis Pass. The bridge was named for County Commissioner Jimmy Vacek. The pass is a popular camping and fishing spot, but the current can be dangerous here.*

Opposite center: *St. Mary's Orphanage was reestablished in this building on Avenue Q at 41st Street after the 1900 storm destroyed the original buildings. The orphanage closed in 1967. Galveston College took over this building. The school is a tax-supported junior college. Galveston voters approved the idea in 1935, but they did not get around to approving the tax until 1966.*

Opposite bottom: *Galveston College also got one of the old buildings at Fort Crockett when the government was disposing of the property there. This was the fort hospital.*

Above: *The government sold part of the Fort Crockett property for commercial development and gave some to local government agencies and kept this row of buildings to house the National Marine Fisheries Service of the Department of Commerce. So much of the real estate in Galveston is owned by government entities that the tax burden on other owners is quite heavy. Galvestonians voted in 1979 to limit increases in city spending to 7 percent per year.*

215

Left: *The Texas Maritime Academy started as a branch of the Texas A&M University system in 1962 in this building on the Fort Crockett grounds.*

Below: *George Mitchell donated a large site on Pelican Island in 1968 and the Moody Foundation granted the school $1 million. The school moved to the new campus on Pelican Island in 1971 and became the College of Marine Sciences and Maritime Resources. The name was changed to Moody College of Marine Sciences and Maritime Resources in 1973. It is now Texas A&M University, Galveston, and this is the only city with branches of both the University of Texas and Texas A&M.*

in the city since the late 1970s. The next census is likely to show the population increasing again.

The state bought the Maco Stewart heirs' life interest in the old Stewart ranch on the west end of the island in 1970 and turned it into the Galveston Island State Park. The Moody family regained full control of the Moody Foundation when the courts ruled there should be just three trustees: Mary Moody Northen and two others named by her.

The Galveston Island State Park is on what was the Maco Stewart Ranch. The old Stewart ranch house is owned now by George Mitchell. He intends to restore it and probably make it a part of the adjacent Galveston Country Club.

Top: *The University includes the Moody College of Marine Technology, offering courses in marine biology and marine sciences, and the Texas Maritime College, offering training toward careers in the Merchant Marine. Students in the Maritime College get some of their training on a ship on loan from the Maritime Administration. This was once the American Export Line's merchantman* Excambion. *It is now called the* Texas Clipper *and it is painted maroon and white, of course.*

Center: *The State Parks and Wildlife Department acquired 1,000 acres on the west end of the island from the Stewart family in 1970. This property extends from the beach to the bay. It is now the Galveston Island State Park with picnic shelters and camp sites and a beach with no motor traffic on it. Included in the park is the Mary Moody Northen Amphitheater, where dramatic programs are presented during the summer months.*

Top: *Galveston has no freeway loop system, so the mall phenomenon has not been as pronounced here as it has been in some other cities. But there are some suburban shopping centers. In 1970, two blocks of Postoffice Street were closed to traffic. The street was filled in and landscaped and a pedestrian shopping mall was created between 21st Street and 23rd Street, right downtown. It has not caught on yet. About one-third of the shops are vacant.*

Right: *The American National Insurance Company completed a new building in 1972 on the block bound by 19th, Market, 20th and Mechanic. It still dominates the skyline of the city.*

A small group of Galvestonians pushed the city into saving the J.M. Brown house in 1971. This is the Broadway mansion better known as Ashton Villa. Brown's granddaughter had sold the house to the El Mina Shrine in 1927. The Shriners wanted a bigger temple by 1968. They tried to sell the house. It had not sold and the Shriners were threatening to tear it down so they could build something bigger on the same site when the city stepped in. Most of the $125,000 it took to buy the house came from the Moody

Foundation, the Kempner Foundation, the Historical Foundation and the federal Department of Housing and Urban Development, but the city holds the title. The Junior League had restored the First National Bank Building and the Trueheart-Adriance Building in 1970 and 1971, but the Galveston Historical Foundation and the drive to save and restore old Galveston buildings really began with Ashton Villa.

Dr. M.L. Ross was mayor in 1971. The Texas Maritime Academy moved to the present Mitchell Campus on Pelican Island. The school changed its name soon afterward to Moody College of Marine Sciences and Maritime Resources. It is a branch of Texas A&M. The American National Insurance Company completed a new building in 1972. The Anico Tower is the tallest building on the island. There is an observation deck open to visitors on the top floor.

The Historical Foundation hired Washington lawyer Peter Brink to be the foundation's executive director. The Moody Foundation established a fund in 1973 to help the

The original immigration station for Galveston was on the east end of the main island. The U.S. Immigration Service built a new station on Pelican Island in 1911. It was damaged by the 1915 hurricane and then reduced to a Public Health Inspection Station. The government closed the inspection station in 1950 and sold the property to the city. It was turned into a park, but it was not easily accessible until 1958 when the bridge to Pelican Island was completed. Seawolf Park was developed on the old quarantine station site. It opened in 1974. The pavilion offers a view of all the ships in the Galveston, Houston and Texas City channels.

Historical Foundation buy and preserve historic buildings. The foundation's method has been to buy buildings and then sell them with covenants requiring the buyers to restore them without altering their appearance. R.A. Apffel was mayor in 1973.

Work started in 1974 to deepen the channel again. The channel was forty feet deep when this work was completed in 1975. The harbor could handle almost anything afloat except the supertankers. Officials of the Galveston Wharves have proposed a terminal for supertankers on Pelican Island. The proposal weathered a referendum, but it is still mired in environmental red tape. Seawolf Park opened in 1974 on the tip of Pelican Island, where the old quarantine station had been. It is a small park with a pavilion, two retired warships and a fishing pier.

The Galveston Historical Foundation bought the old iron sailing bark *Elissa* in 1974. The *Elissa* was in a shipyard in Greece and about to be turned into scrap when the foundation's agents rescued her. The *Elissa* had been converted

to a motor ship years earlier. Foundation employees and volunteers patched her up and towed her to Galveston in 1979 and started restoring her. The hull had to have a major operation. The masts and all the rigging had to be made from scratch. The restoration was far enough along by 1982 that the *Elissa* was able to go sailing in the Gulf on Labor Day.

Galveston abandoned the promotion of Splash Day completely after a few episodes in the 1960s when hordes of students from the mainland celebrated the opening of the beach season by staging riots. The islanders went through a period when they seemed to be hoping the tourists would go somewhere else, but mainlanders continued to build summer houses on the west end of the island and they began to make investments in the city. There are better beaches than Galveston's, but there is no beach closer to Houston. Mainlanders were investing in this reality while the islanders were still hoping no one would notice.

The Con-Del Company of Dallas built the first high-rise

Opposite top left: *The World War II submarine* Cavalla *and the destroyer escort* Stewart *are open to visitors in Seawolf Park. The park is named for one of the U.S. submarines lost in World War II.*

Opposite top right: *Galveston County has acquired the old Army coastal artillery base on Bolivar Point and it is now a county park. This was Fort Travis. The guns are gone, but the fortifications are still here.*

Opposite bottom left: *The link between Galveston and Bolivar is the free ferry system operated by the Texas Department of Highways and Public Transportation. The trip across the channel entrance takes fifteen minutes. There is plenty of free parking at the landing for people* interested just in riding over and back without their cars.

Opposite bottom right: *The Galveston ferry landing is right alongside the Coast Guard Station where the cutters that used to chase the rumrunners were based. The coast guardsmen occasionally intercept a boat load of marijuana these days.*

condominium apartment building on the beach in 1974. Nat Shapiro of Houston built the second one, on the seawall, in 1975. Dr. Denton Cooley and Archie Bennett of Houston bought the old Galvez Hotel in 1978 and restored it. John Unbehagen was mayor.

Houstonians and doctors working at the University of Texas Medical Branch have taken a leading role in the restoration of the city's old homes. The biggest single investor in Galveston property in the past twenty years has been George Mitchell. He is the head of an oil empire based in Houston, but he was born in Galveston. Mitchell and his wife and his companies own more real estate on the island than anyone else. Mitchell says he is sure Galveston has a great future as a tourist resort. He and his brothers grew up in Galveston during the Maceos' heyday. George Mitchell did not join in the campaign for legalizing gambling in 1984. The Historical Foundation opposed it. Islanders voted two to one against legal casinos in the referendum held January 21.

Top left: *Galvestonians were slow to take to beachfront condominiums. There were many of them on the Florida coast and on Padre Island before the first one was built here in 1974. The first one was built by a Dallas developer and called Islander East. It came through Hurricane Alicia without serious damage.*

Top right: *The 1983 hurricane did do some damage to By the Sea Condominiums on the seawall. A Houston developer built this one in 1975.*

Below left: *The Galvestonian was unfinished and unoccupied when Hurricane Alicia struck. This is a $30 million project. Dr. Ed Henderson of Galveston is a partner in it with Jim Schindler of Houston.*

Below right: *Smaller condominium projects along the seawall suffered substantial damage during the 1983 hurricane. This prompted the Galveston City Council to begin considering whether the building codes should be more stringent.*

Opposite top: *Many of the new apartment and condominium projects along the seawall are on the site where the Municipal Golf Course was before the city sold it to developers in 1972.*

The old residents and old institutions warmed up very slowly to the idea of turning the old sections of town into tourist attractions. Mary Moody Northen and the Moody Foundation were about the first. The original Moody contributions to the Historical Foundation's preservation fund were fairly modest, but the commitment gradually grew to proportions befitting the foundation's own history and character. Moody money paid for most of the cost of restoring and outfitting the *Elissa*. Moody money restored the

Galveston has made a couple of good trades with golf courses. The original Municipal Golf Course was on Offatt's Bayou. It opened in 1932. The federal government bought that course in 1942 as part of the expansion of the air base. The city used the $75,000 it got in that deal to make the down payment on the Galveston Country Club property at 61st Street and Seawall after the war. The city sold the 61st Street property to real estate developers in 1972 and then developed the present Municipal Golf Course on a bayside site that had been part of the airbase.

Top left: *George Mitchell and his wife, Cynthia, and the Mitchell companies are now the largest landowners on Galveston Island. The Mitchells have oil and gas interests on the island and offshore. They have resort subdivisions and several million dollars' worth of restoration projects in the historic district.*

Top right: *Mitchell also is building a new hotel and condominium project on part of old Fort Crockett. He is incorporating into the San Luis landscaping the casemates where the twelve-inch guns once were housed. There is another major condominium underway on the seawall and another in the medical center. The city has been encouraging such development with tax reinvestment zones and other incentives. Building permit totals rose from $22.5 million in 1981 to $54 million in 1982, not including university and port projects.*

Center: *Galvestonians believe in referendums. They forced one when the Wharves Board decided to demolish old Pier 19 and build a new pier and warehouse in its place. The vote saved the pier that is the home of about half the Galveston shrimp fleet.*

Bottom: *The Hill family had a fish market at the edge of Pier 19 before the referendum. The Hills added an eating establishment after the vote. The sign says it is a restaurant. But it is cafeteria style. All the windows on the back look out on the shrimp boat basin. The seafood is as fresh as you can get.*

226

Top right: *Galveston got a new editorial voice in 1977 when Steven Long and two associates started publishing* In Between. *It is a free tabloid newspaper featuring gossip, opinion and a large measure of history,published every other Thursday.*

Above: *The John Sealy Hospital has grown into one of the major medical centers in the state, and it is still growing. Clusters of modern buildings stand now where the original hospital building Nicholas Clayton designed stood.*

Bottom: *The Texas Legislature has heard suggestions more than once that the University of Texas Medical Branch should be moved somewhere else. The factor, more than any other, that has kept the school here is the support the school's hospital gets from the Sealy-Smith Foundation. John Sealy, Jr. and his sister, Mrs. R.W. Smith, established the foundation to support the hospital their father endowed. The foundation has put millions into the hospital and medical center.*

Right: *Galveston has saved more of its past than most cities have. But the building that housed the Maceos' Turf Athletic Club, Studio Lounge and Western Room is gone forever. That building and all the other buildings in the 2200 block of Market were demolished to clear a site for what is now the Interfirst Bank. This is the old First Hutchings, Sealy Bank, incorporating the old Commercial and Agricultural Bank, the Ball, Hutchings Company, the Hutchings, Sealy Company, the Galveston Bank and Trust Company, the Henry Rosenberg Bank, the South Texas State Bank, the South Texas National Bank and the First National.*

Left: *St. Mary's Hospital has outgrown the Nicholas Clayton building where it once was housed. The last section of the building that was a refuge for so many Galvestonians during the 1900 storm was demolished in the 1970s and St. Mary's now occupies this modern building on the original site, across the street from John Sealy.*

Santa Fe Building and built the railroad museum there.

Gus Manuel was elected mayor in 1979.

The Wharves Board had been talking for years about tearing down old Pier 19 and putting up a big new wharf and warehouse on the site. Pier 19 is the pier where the charter boats and about half the Galveston shrimp fleet berth. It is just a block from the center of the old Strand district, where the Historical Foundation's restoration efforts are concentrated.

Top: *The only downtown Galveston bank still independent and still owned by Galvestonians is the Moody National at Postoffice and 23rd Street, incorporating the old Texas Bank and Insurance Company, the Galveston National Bank and the City National.*

Below: *Shearn Moody, Jr. was running the venerable W.L. Moody and Company private bank when it got into difficulties and closed in 1972. The building at Church and 23rd has been standing vacant ever since. This is the corner where the Tremont Hotel stood until 1928.*

Top: *Cotton was the commodity that propelled Galveston into prominence as a port. But the cotton business has changed drastically. Cotton is now pressed and stored in the growing areas. Increasing quantities of cotton are shipped overland to the West Coast for export to the Orient. Galveston's port business is more diversified today. This is a major grain port and container shipments are increasingly important.*

Below left: *Willie Socha pours the coffee when the Sunday Morning Coffee Club meets on the Galveston beach. Socha was not born on the island, but many of the members of the coffee club were. The members are influental civic and business leaders and office holders. They exchange views about the city and its problems and opportunities for an hour every Sunday morning at a beachfront spot called Christie's Beachcomber.*

Below right: *The Beachcomber was the home base of the late Galveston promoter, columnist and bon vivant, Christie Mitchell. Christie was the older brother of Johnny and George Mitchell. The Mitchell brothers and their sister Maria all were born on the island. Their parents were Greek immigrants. Mitchell is the name they adopted after they settled here.*

Pier 19 also has been a banana wharf for generations. It is literally falling down. The people running the wharves wanted to move the shrimp boats and party boats to Pelican Island and build a first-class new dock.

The Historical Foundation was not able to get the decision changed any other way; so the foundation's partisans petitioned for a referendum. Galveston voters sided with the Historical Foundation. The political wind was blowing from a new direction. Hill's Fish Market celebrated by

Above left: *Nicholas Clayton's widow grieved because she could not afford a suitable marker for Clayton's grave when he died in 1916. This marker finally was placed over Clayton's grave in Calvary Cemetery on June 11, 1983. That day was observed by Galveston historical organizations as Nicholas Clayton Day.*

Above right: *Nicholas Clayton's daughter Mary unveiled the marker. She had a long career as a commercial photographer in Galveston and she still lives on the island.*

Below: *Most of Clayton's living descendants attended the Clayton Day ceremonies. Nicholas J. Clayton III and Nicholas J. Clayton IV came from their home in Louisiana. They are pictured here on The Strand where many of the early buildings designed by Clayton have recently been restored.*

Top: *It took several years for the restoration movement to gain much momentum. Emily Whiteside was one of the first to get interested. She renovated these commercial buildings in 1974 and turned them into fashionable flats. The buildings were built in 1870 on 23rd Street just off Mechanic for Rice, Boulard and Company.*

Center: *Another early project was the restoration of the old Produce Building on The Strand, now the home of the Old Strand Emporium wine, cheese and snack shop.*

Bottom: *Buildings that were in danger of falling down a short time ago are being restored now all along The Strand and Mechanic Street and throughout the three main historic districts. The historical foundation has a consultant on the staff to advise people restoring old buildings.*

232

adding a restaurant to the market building on Pier 19.

The shrimp boats and the charter boats still berth at Pier 19. The *Elissa* is moored nearby. The scene is picturesque, but the old banana wharf is still falling down. The Wharves Board has not given up the idea of a new dock. The board in 1983 commissioned a consulting firm to study the waterfront area adjacent to the Strand Historic District, from Pier 19 to Pier 25. The consultants have recommended moving the banana business to another dock and converting all the

Top: *This home, designed by Charles Bulger and built in 1889 on 17th Street just off Postoffice, is now a small hotel, offering bed and breakfast for tourists interested in seeing Galveston the way it was.*

Bottom: *The Galveston Historical Foundation staged a street festival in 1974 for foundation members and supporters. Everybody had such a good time that the festival became an annual event. It is called Dickens's Evening on The Strand. It is usually the first Saturday and Sunday in December.*

Above: *John's Oyster Resort on the Freeway at Offatt's Bayou has even been renovated. This is said to be the oldest restaurant on the island. It looked its age before the new owners fixed it up in the spring of 1983.*

Below: *Tourist interest in the old buildings and historic neighborhoods is increasing. The Treasure Isle Tour Train is usually filled during the tourist season. The Tour Train depot is Moody Center on the seawall.*

Opposite: *The beach still is the island's number one attraction. East beach between Broadway and the jetties is the most popular. Real Galvestonians almost never come here during the tourist season.*

Top left: *The interest in restoring old buildings has spread well beyond the historic districts. The old Y.W.C.A. Building across 21st Street from the courthouse was vacant for years until developer J.R. McConnell bought it and turned it into an office complex. The building McConnell renamed Jackson Square opened in 1983.*

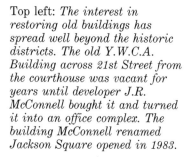

area around Pier 19 into an entertainment complex with restaurants and a shopping mall and maybe hotels. It is the first time the people concerned with keeping the port up to date and the people trying to preserve the city's nineteenth century landmarks have appeared to be moving in the same direction. It could be another turning point comparable to the rescue of Ashton Villa.

Residents of the west end area beyond the end of the seawall almost all left as Hurricane Alicia began to threaten Galveston on August 17, 1983. Ninety percent of the residents of the city proper stayed and rode out the storm in their homes or in emergency shelters. Many summer homes on the west end were demolished. Part of the beach and all the dunes washed away. There was heavy damage to some buildings in the city, but they were nearly all still standing when the storm passed. Galvestonians by the afternoon of the eighteenth were beginning to make repairs. The sun was shining on their island again by the nineteenth. Galveston had survived one more hurricane.

ACKNOWLEDGEMENTS

The author is indebted to many individuals and institutions for assistance. Particularly valuable was the unselfish and generous advice and counsel of Bob Nesbitt. Jane Kenamore and Uli Haller of Galveston's Rosenberg Library were especially helpful. Doris Glasser, Carol Lee and Douglas Weiskopf of the Texas and Local History Room of the Houston Public Library assisted in research and suggested sources for photographs. Thanks also to Ralph Elder of the Eugene C. Barker Texas History Center at The University of Texas at Austin, to Jane Chapin of Galveston and to Judy King of Houston.

Some of the publications worthy of recommendation to readers wishing more information are:

Albert Lasker, The Man Who Shaped a Century: John Gunther.
Bob's Galveston Island Reader: Bob Nesbitt.
Coin of Contraband: Robert Roark.
Death from the Sea: Herbert Molloy Mason, Jr.
Every Kind of Ship Work: C. Bradford Mitchell.
Fishing the Texas Coast: A.C. Becker, Jr.
Galveston, A Different Place: Virginia Eisenhour.
Galveston Era, The: Earl W. Fornell.
Galveston in a Nutshell: Galveston Business League, 1904.
Galveston in 1900: edited by Clarence Ousley.
Galveston 1910: Greater Galveston Publicity Committee.
Galveston That Was, The: Howard Barnstone.
Great Galveston Disaster, The: Paul Lester.
Guide to Historic Galveston, A: Douglas Zweiner.
Handbook of Texas, The: Texas State Historical Association.
Hero of Bataan: The Story of General Jonathan M. Wainright: Duane Schultz.

History of the Island and the City of Galveston: Charles W. Hayes.

Hurricane Carla: Warren L. Hogan.

Indianola, Mother of Western Texas: Brownson Malsch.

Informal History of the First Baptist Church, Galveston, Texas, An: Vernon Bennett.

King Vidor: John Baxter.

Maco Stewart: Lewis Valentine Ulrey.

Port of Galveston Calendars, 1970, 1976 & 1978: Bob Nesbitt.

Sociological Study of a Segregated District, A: Granville Price.

Stone and Webster Public Service Journal, Vol. 4, No. 2. & Vol. 12, No. 4.

Story of the Galveston Disaster: Walter B. Stevens.

Three Quarters of a Century of Progress: W.L. Moody and Co., Bankers, 1941.

Texas Almanac.

Texas Almanac Compendium of Texas History, 1857-1873: edited by James Day.

Treasures of Galveston Bay: Carroll Lewis.

Weekend in September: John Edward Weems.

William Bollaert's Texas.

PHOTO CREDITS

The color photographs for this book were made by Robert John Mihovil with the exception of the NASA photograph on page 38. The black and white photographs were made by the author except for those listed below. The author and the publisher wish to express their gratitude and appreciation to these individuals and organizations for permitting the reproduction of photographs from their collections:

American National Insurance Company, 196 (upper)
Bastrop Historical Society, 44
Bob Nesbitt, xiii (lower), 74 (right), 74 (bottom), 105, 119, 165, 166, 171 (lower), 175 (upper), 177, 182, 186 (center), 186 (lower), 190 (upper)
Channel 11, 197 (lower)
Christie's Beachcomber, 7, 8, 9, 11, 15, 178, 179, 204 (upper), 230 (lower right)
Ed Bourdon, 20 (lower)
First Baptist Church of Galveston, 149 (lower)
Galveston Historical Foundation, 233 (lower)
Galveston Isle Magazine, 12, 17
Galveston News, 5 (upper), 16, 18, 19, 138, 163 (right), 172 (lower), 191 (upper), 222 (upper left)
In Between, 162 (lower)
J.D. Burnette, 208
Jill Devoti, 168
Johnny Goyen, 43
Metropolitan Research Center, Houston Public Library, 5 (lower), 14, 46, 56, 59 (left), 74 (upper), 83, 89, 99 (right), 114, 117 (lower), 124 (lower left), 136 (upper), 139, 144, 147, 148, 150 (lower), 150 (right), 151, 152 (upper), 152 (lower), 153, 160 (lower), 163 (lower), 164, 167 (lower), 172 (upper), 207 (upper & lower), 227 (lower)

INDEX

Bold type indicates the location of a related photograph.

242

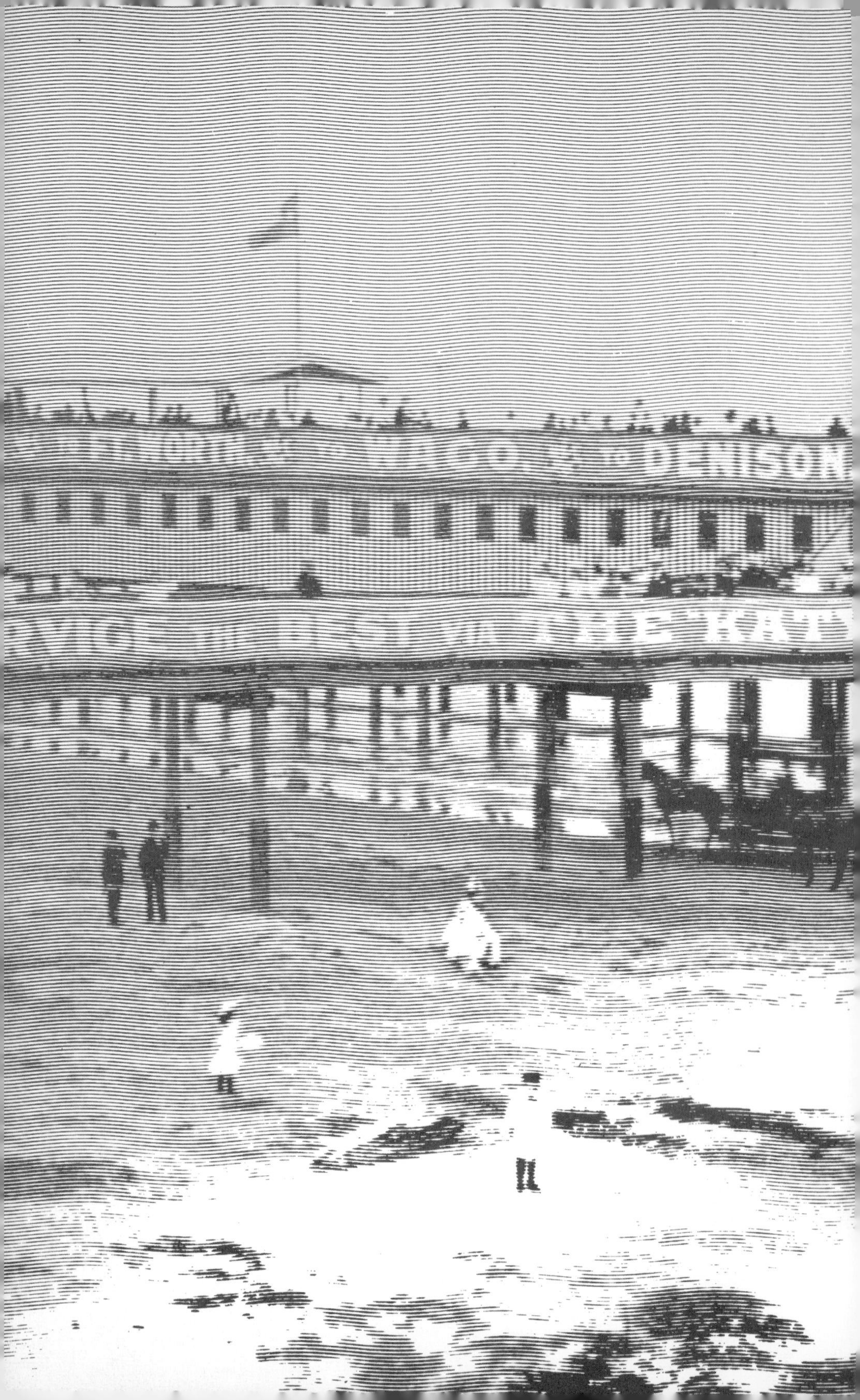
DENISON